THE STANSBERRY RESEARCH
STARTER'S
GUIDE
FOR NEW INVESTORS

By Stansberry Research

Published by Stansberry Research

Edited by Fawn Gwynallen and Justin Dove

About Stansberry Research

Founded in 1999 and based out of Baltimore, Maryland, Stansberry Research is the largest independent source of financial insight in the world. It delivers unbiased investment advice to self-directed investors seeking an edge in a wide variety of sectors and market conditions.

Stansberry Research has nearly two dozen analysts and researchers – including former hedge-fund managers and buy-side financial experts. They produce a steady stream of timely research on value investing, income generation, resources, biotech, financials, short-selling, macroeconomic analysis, options trading, and more.

The company's unrelenting and uncompromised insight has made it one of the most respected and sought-after research organizations in the financial sector. It has nearly one million readers and more than 500,000 paid subscribers in over 100 countries.

About the Contributors

Porter Stansberry

Porter Stansberry founded Stansberry Research in 1999 with the firm's flagship newsletter, *Stansberry's Investment Advisory*. He is also the host of Stansberry Radio, a weekly podcast that is one of the most popular online financial radio shows.

Prior to launching Stansberry Research, Porter was the first American editor of the *Fleet Street Letter*, the world's oldest English-language financial newsletter.

Today, Porter is well-known for doing some of the most important – and often controversial – work in the financial-advisory business. Since he launched *Stansberry's Investment Advisory*, his string of accurate forecasts has made his advisory one of the most widely read in the world... and has helped his readers both avoid catastrophe and make incredible gains.

Brian Hunt

 Brian Hunt is the Editor in Chief of Stansberry Research.

Since 2007, he has managed dozens of Stansberry Research's investment newsletters and trading advisories, helping make Stansberry Research one of the largest financial publishers in the world.

Brian is a successful private trader and frequently contributes to *Growth Stock Wire*, *DailyWealth*, and *The Stansberry Digest*. He is the co-founder of *DailyWealth Trader*, one of the world's most popular and highly regarded trading advisories.

Brian is also the co-author of the book *High Income Retirement: How to Safely Earn 12%-20% Income Streams on Your Savings*.

Dr. David Eifrig, Jr.

Dr. Eifrig is the editor of three Stansberry Research newsletters... *Retirement Millionaire* shows readers how to live a millionaire lifestyle on less money than you'd imagine possible. *Retirement Trader* shows readers a safe way to double or triple the gains in their retirement account with less risk. *Income Intelligence* shows investors how to expertly time their purchases to maximize their returns.

Doc has one of the best track records in the financial-newsletter business. From 2010 to 2014, he closed 136 winning positions in a row for his *Retirement Trader* subscribers.

Before joining Stansberry Research in 2008, Dr. Eifrig worked in arbitrage and trading groups with major Wall Street investment banks, including Goldman Sachs, Chase Manhattan, and Yamaichi in Japan. He is also a board-eligible ophthalmologist.

Dan Ferris

Dan Ferris is the editor of *Extreme Value*, a monthly investment advisory that focuses on the safest stocks in the market: great businesses trading at steep discounts...

Dan joined Stansberry Research in 2000. In 2002, he became the editor of *Extreme Value*. His strategy of finding safe, cheap, and profitable stocks has earned him a loyal following... He counts more than 20 major financial firms and well-known fund managers as subscribers. And he has built one of the most impressive track records in the industry.

Longtime *Extreme Value* readers have enjoyed a long list of double- and triple-digit winners thanks to Dan's diligent research, including Gateway (124%), Blair Corp (111%), KHD Humboldt Wedag (249%), International Royalty (248%), Portfolio Recovery Associates (104%), Alexander & Baldwin (201%), and Encana (171%), among many others.

As a result of his work in *Extreme Value*, Dan has been featured several times in *Barron's*, the *Value Investing Letter*, and financial radio and TV programs around the country.

Steve Sjuggerud

Dr. Steve Sjuggerud is the editor of *True Wealth*, which focuses on safe, unique, alternative investments overlooked by Wall Street. He is also the editor of *True Wealth Systems*, which has distilled decades of Steve's investing experience into three dozen computer trading models.

Prior to joining Stansberry Research in 2001, Steve was a stockbroker, vice president of a global mutual fund, and head of a hedge fund. He has been quoted by the *Wall Street Journal*, *Barron's*, and the *Washington Post*. He also co-authored *Safe Strategies for Financial Freedom*, a bestselling book on investment strategies. He holds a doctorate in finance.

Guest Contributor

Mark Ford

Mark Ford is the editor of *The Palm Beach Letter*, which offers advice on building wealth, living well, and investing.

Mark started his first business when he was 11 years old. In the decades since then, he has started hundreds more and been involved in the development of dozens of multimillion-dollar businesses.

In 1982, Mark worked as an apprentice to a well-known businessman in South Florida. He helped the man's small publishing company grow to $135 million in annual revenues, became a multi-millionaire himself, and retired at age 39.

Mark has written a dozen books on entrepreneurship, personal productivity, and wealth building. Three of these were *New York Times* and *Wall Street Journal* bestsellers.

Table of Contents

Introduction

By Brian Hunt

Starting out as an investor is intimidating.

Spend a few minutes in the investment section of a bookstore or watch a financial television program, and you'll encounter at least a dozen market strategies and "gurus." It's information overload.

If you're new to investing – or new to the Stansberry Research family – it can be overwhelming. We feature numerous investment experts... each with their own strategies and beliefs.

Although our research products feature different styles of investing, all our services are rooted in the same intellectual principles. We believe these principles are vital to successful wealth building.

In *The Stansberry Research Starter's Guide for New Investors*, we've identified 10 core concepts that are vital to successful wealth building and investment.

We feature educational essays and interviews from Stansberry Research editors and trusted advisers that will educate you on each of those 10 concepts... and why they're so important for amateur and master investors alike to understand.

These are the ideas we wish we'd learned before we invested a single dollar. Take them to heart, and you can ignore just about everything else.

Becoming a successful investor is a long journey. But this guide can greatly reduce the time it takes to travel it.

Regards,

Brian Hunt
Editor in Chief
Stansberry Research

Realize That the Surest Road to Wealth Is Not Through Your Investments

It's a truth many people don't want to believe: *You're unlikely to achieve tremendous wealth through investing alone.*

Sure, there are rare exceptions... but for the vast majority of us, the best way to achieve wealth is to build a successful business or become a highly paid employee... *then save a large portion of your earnings rather than spend it.*

Only once you've mastered the "earn... then save instead of spend" mentality should you move on to investing.

In the following pages, you'll find several ideas that will help you earn and save a lot of money...

How to Get a Raise at Work

An interview with Mark Ford

Editor Mark Ford has built a reputation as one of the country's foremost experts on wealth building.

But unlike most "experts" in this field, Mark actually walks the walk. He's a serial entrepreneur and *New York Times* bestselling author who has built dozens of businesses... and a huge personal fortune.

Mark spends his time with family, mentoring entrepreneurs, and managing his investments. He also shares his unconventional wealth ideas with people through books and financial newsletters, like his *Palm Beach Letter*.

For our money, nobody in America delivers no-B.S. financial advice as well as Mark Ford. In the following interview, you'll get Mark's best advice for people looking to increase their income...

———————●———————

Stansberry Research: Mark, you're a successful entrepreneur... a highly paid consultant... and an accomplished writer. You've also built a reputation as one of the country's foremost experts on wealth building.

For many people, the biggest source of potential wealth is their salary.

You've said that earning just a few percentage points more each year will help you become a millionaire by the time you retire.

Could you explain how to get a raise... and how it can make a huge difference to a person's long-term wealth?

Mark Ford: Absolutely... There's no question about it. Earning just a few percentage points more each year can make you much, much richer over a lifetime.

To show you how, let me start with an example...

My brother hired SP for $20,000. On the same day, he hired LJ for $30,000. Keep in mind... I'm using initials to avoid embarrassing these people. They both had the same qualifications: college degrees, a bit of experience interning for investment companies, and the desire to make a lot of money.

SP stood out from day one. He was the first one to work every morning and stayed after everyone else, including my brother, went home at night. LJ was good but rather ordinary.

Flash-forward 13 years. SP is making more than $2 million every year and LJ is making $38,000.

SP has already outpaced LJ by more than $10 million. By the time they both retire, SP will have a net worth well in excess of $50 million, while LJ will be lucky if he has anything in his bank account.

Stansberry Research: What accounted for the difference?

Ford: It was not intelligence. It was simply the fact that SP decided to become a superstar while LJ was content to be ordinary.

That's how I see it. But let me try to prove it to you with some simple arithmetic.

Joe Ordinary is 25 years old, makes an ordinary $30,000-per-year income and gets ordinary 3.5% yearly increases. Over a 40-year career, he will make a little more than $2.6 million.

Sarah Superstar, also 25, averages 5% yearly increases. Over the same 40-year period, she will earn $3.8 million – over $1 million more than Joe.

If Sarah can keep her expenditures down and live on the same amount of money that Joe is making, she will retire a millionaire while Joe will be forced to live on food stamps and handouts.

That's how big a difference a mere 1.5 percentage points can make when we're talking about raises.

And that 1.5% difference, from the studies I've read, is what Sarah can expect by working hard and making smart decisions throughout her career.

Stansberry Research: Is there a plan someone can follow to achieve that "extra" 1.5%?

Ford: There is... and if you stick with it, you could become a multimillionaire in no more than 20 years. But there's something even more exciting than that. Your path to wealth must start somewhere. So in addition to that "blueprint," I can also give you a plan to get an increase of at least 10% one year from now...

Stansberry Research: To most people, that sounds almost too good to be true. Where do we begin?

Ford: Let's start by taking a look at how salaries work in a typical business environment.

Businesses exist to provide products and services to consumers. Healthy businesses measure their success in terms of their long-term profits.

As an employee of a business, it's your job to help your company produce those long-term profits. You may think your job is something other than that. You may think, for example, that your job is to answer the phone or deliver the mail or write marketing copy. Nothing could be further from the truth. Your job is to produce long-term profits.

The secret to getting above-average raises each year is to accept that as your fundamental responsibility – and to transform the work you are doing now in such a way that it will produce those long-term profits. The better you can do it, the more money you will make. It's as simple as that.

Salespeople generally make more than accountants, right?

That's not because salespeople are smarter than accountants. Nor do they necessarily work harder. But the job they do is seen as more financially valuable than the job accountants do. That is the one and only reason they get paid more.

Stansberry Research: What if you are working as a low-ranking employee right now?

Ford: I would tell you not to worry. My plan works just as well for a low-ranking employee as it does for top brass. In fact, it works better.

Conventional business roles and conventional salaries are the reality for 80% of the workforce – for people who come to work and put in a full day and have a good attitude and hope for the best.

For most of the other 20% – people who are smart and willing to work harder – the business world will reward them with better raises and more in total earnings over a 40-year period.

But there is a smaller group of employees – maybe 25% of that 20% (or 4% of the whole) – who will average even higher raises. Those employees will also earn far more throughout their business careers... enough to make it possible for them to retire rich.

There are more than a dozen employees I've worked with personally during the past 20 years who have taken this less-traveled road. None of them are older than 45 (most are in their 30s), and they are already all multimillionaires.

If they continue as they have been – and there is no reason why they shouldn't – they will all be among the top one-half of 1% of the population in wealth when they decide to retire.

Stansberry Research: So let's talk about how someone can make that happen for himself.

Ford: Start with this: Make a commitment to become the most valuable employee in your department in six months and the most valuable employee in your boss' view in one year.

These two goals are not necessarily synonymous. As you may already know, what your boss thinks about you and who you are may be two different things. The first job of anyone who wants to become a superstar is to actually start doing more valuable work. The second job is to gradually let your boss (and your boss' bosses) know that.

Make that commitment now.

Then make a list of all the ways you are currently valuable to your boss. And then make another list of things you can do to increase your value.

That list will be a good source of ideas for you. Let's say you implement this plan at the start of the year. In January, for example, you might make it a point to get your boss his most important report a day earlier than normal. In February, you might tell him he can delegate to you the sales calls he hates to make.

If you use a daily task list, you should be making great progress by the spring and have completely upgraded your responsibilities by the middle of the year. Now is the time to start letting your boss know about your achievements (in the event that he hasn't noticed already).

Guide all of your business decisions by one sole criterion: How will this action help my company increase its long-term profitability?

Meanwhile, be sure to stay humble and credit other people for their assistance when they have, in fact, helped you.

Be conscious of your boss' ego, too. Give him credit whenever anyone compliments you on some achievement. A statement as simple as "I couldn't have done it without Jeff's help/wisdom" will usually do the trick.

And take the time to write your boss and key fellow employees the occasional memo thanking them for their help.

By following a two-tier strategy – contributing more to the business and making friends along the way – you will ensure that your path to success will be quick and easy.

As your responsibilities increase, your boss will begin to depend on you.

Eventually – and this may happen in six months, or it may take a year – he will see you as an entirely different and more important employee than any of the others he deals with. He will begin to think of you as indispensable.

At that point, you should have no trouble getting your 10% raise. You might do much better than that.

Stansberry Research: Is there anything else an employee should do to make sure they get that raise?

Ford: Yes... and it's very important not to skip this step.

Establish relationships with other employees who have a higher rank than you. Ask them for their help and insight. Volunteer to help them do their jobs, and do that work after hours.

Your goal is to develop a back-up network of powerful people who see you as an up-and-comer. These people can be instrumental in getting you the raise you deserve if your boss, for whatever reason, fails to give you your due.

If you can, develop relationships with colleagues from other businesses in your industry, too. You never know – a few of them may offer you more than 10% to come and work for them.

Here's a key point: The habits you have to work on now to get yourself that 10% raise will be the same habits that will help you double or triple your salary in the future. Superstar employees don't do 100 things better than ordinary, good employees. They usually do just a handful. You'll discover and perfect your handful next year in seeking to please your boss, and you'll be able to use those new skills to go all the way to the top.

Stansberry Research: But what if the actions you have to take to please your boss are not the best thing for the business?

Ford: I receive this question often. Some businesses – and this happens more frequently with larger, corporate businesses than with growing enterprises – become politically divided. In such businesses, it's possible to get a job working for someone who cares more about himself and his own power than about the company's future.

If you have such a boss, you should really try to find a better one. But if you can't, you will have to be a bit duplicitous. You will have to do everything you can to please him while you are carrying out your plan. But at the same time, find someone else in the company, someone with power, who is willing to mentor you.

That person will be either one of your boss' equals or one of his bosses. Most importantly, he must be someone who is committed to the company's long-term profitability. Remember, that is the bottom-line measuring stick for the success of any business.

Work to please your mentor at the same time as you work to please your boss. By pleasing your boss, you'll get your big raise next year. And by pleasing your mentor, you eventually will be able to abandon your boss' rotten ship and secure a much better position.

Stansberry Research: All great advice. Any closing thoughts?

Ford: The greater your contribution to your company's success, the higher the salary you will demand. And the best way to be a big contributor is to practice a financially valuable skill.

There aren't a whole lot of financially valuable business skills to choose from. It's good to know how to analyze a spreadsheet or engineer a new design. But if you want to make dramatically more money than you're making now, you are almost certainly going to have to start doing at least one of the three things businesses traditionally pay big bucks for: selling, marketing, and/or managing profits.

You've probably heard this before… and you might be thinking this advice does not apply to you because you don't work in a sales or marketing role.

That's not the case at all…

You don't need to change your profession to contribute a financially valuable skill to your employer. While you work as an accountant or lawyer or engineer, work also with the sales and marketing team to find out how you can help them.

Do this voluntarily. Make friends and connections. Do honest and good work for them. Eventually, you will be seen as someone who can step up to take a senior position.

I know two accountants, three lawyers, and one engineer who did that. I also know a data-input operator, a proofreader, and a customer-service person… They are all CEOs or COOs today, making hundreds of thousands with seven-figure net worths…

But even if you choose not to do that, you can and should be able to boost your salary by 10% next year. And here is how you are going to do it:

First, make a resolution to be more valuable to your boss and/or your business. Do it now. Write it down.

Second, make a list of all the ways you are currently valuable to your boss and/or your business.

Third, make a list of a dozen or so ways that you can increase your value to your boss and/or your business. And pick at least one of them as your objective for next month.

And fourth, figure out some way to communicate to your boss or to your company's president that you want to make a bigger contribution this year. (No need to tell him you want a higher salary. He will "get" that without you saying so.)

If you set for yourself the goal of getting a 10% raise next year and you get just half of that, you will still be much richer when you retire than you will be if you ignore this advice and go back to accepting the ordinary.

So please – start with that 10% goal. Decide to be a much better employee in six months and have a network of people in place who understand your value in one year.

Then get that raise and watch your wealth grow.

Stansberry Research: This is all very useful information. Thanks, Mark.

Ford: You're welcome.

Two Simple Rules Everyone Should Know About Money

A discussion with Porter Stansberry

In 2011, Stansberry Research founder Porter Stansberry launched his own radio show. Within three years, it became one of the most popular financial radio shows in America.

The reason for the success of "Stansberry Radio" is simple. Porter consistently delivers great advice for people looking to live a better, wealthier life.

In the radio transcript below, Porter details several key ideas people can use to build significant wealth. He directed his comments toward young people. But these ideas are useful, no matter what your age.

Before you make a single investment, make sure you understand the ideas Porter discusses below...

———————●———————

For the young folks out there, the single most important thing you can learn, at your age, has nothing to do with investing.

It's simply this: **Live beneath your means**. **Do not borrow money**.

It's that simple.

If you just go to work every day, try your best, build a career, save 20%-25% of your income, and don't get into debt... by the time you are 35 years old, you will be well ahead of the game.

By the time you're 40, you can be a millionaire, easily. And you don't have to do anything with investing beyond corporate bonds, municipal bonds, and local real estate deals. There is no reason for you to become a stock trader or an options seller or anything like that. You don't have to do that, and I wouldn't recommend you do it until you can do it full time.

Now, let's say you're 55 years old and you're retiring. You've got 40 hours a week to spend on your investments. Fantastic! You can trade stocks or stock options.

But if you're 20-something right now, don't waste your time and energy with all that stuff...

You can read about it. You can learn about it. That's great. But just focus on increasing your income by building a career and/ or having a part-time business of your own... and living beneath your means.

Now here are some easy things to avoid: Don't ever borrow money to go to college. College is a waste of time to start with. Why would you borrow money to waste time? It makes no sense.

Second – and this is the trap that a lot of people fall into – they want a huge house. They're 28 years old, they're 30 years old... They get married. They have a kid, and they believe, therefore, they've got to have a house – the house. And they go crazy into debt to buy it.

Don't do it. I swear, you don't have to do that. If you just focus, instead, on living within your means, you can buy a small condo. You can live there for five years until you can afford to buy a small house. And by the way, I said "buy." I didn't say "mortgage." I said "buy."

If you become dedicated to never getting into debt, your entire financial life will be brilliantly successful. If you can't avoid the temptation to get into debt, there's a 50%/50% chance that you'll never make it. So what's the best thing you can do to increase your odds of financial success?

Simple. Live within your means and avoid debt.   .

The thing I want to tell young people is that unless you can do it on a full-time basis, you don't need to start investing yet...

Sure, some of your money should go into high-quality, blue-chip, dividend-growing stocks. Absolutely. That's part of your savings program. You can do it via your 401(k). You can do it with an IRA. I'm not saying avoid stocks altogether. But I'm saying most of your money should be in corporate bonds, municipal bonds, gold, silver, and rental real estate.

More importantly, figure out how to avoid being in debt.

There is an easy way to do it. Just say, "I'm not going to borrow money." Then everything else in your life will become a lot simpler. You're not going to be shopping for a new car, for example. You could buy a decent car for $2,000. Why would you borrow $20,000 to buy a new one? It makes no sense.

If you really want to be rich, the first step is: Don't ever borrow a penny. As soon as you understand interest, you will only be a lender. You will never be a borrower.

Out of all the things I did right financially, that was the most important one.

Learn Why Asset Allocation Is the No. 1 Factor in Your Investment Success

The single most important factor in your investing success has nothing to do with picking the right stocks.

It has nothing to do with paying attention to what the president or Congress says. It has nothing to do with the state of the economy. It has nothing to do with knowing how to "time the market."

The single most important factor in your investing success is 100 times more important than any of those things.

Ignorance and mismanagement of this factor ruin more retirements than every other factor combined. Yet most investors never give this idea any thought...

This vitally important idea is called "asset allocation."

If you don't know and practice proper asset allocation, you're almost sure to lose money with your investments.

In the following section, you'll learn all about this timeless idea...

The Single Most Important Factor in Your Investment Success

An interview with Dr. David Eifrig Jr
Editor, *Retirement Millionaire*

No one is more qualified to speak about intelligent asset allocation than Dr. David Eifrig, Jr.

"Doc" is a former professional trader at one of the world's top investment banks. He's also an extremely successful private investor and the editor of the wildly popular *Retirement Millionaire* service.

In the educational interview below, Doc discusses the vital concept of asset allocation... and why it's the critical factor in your investment success.

———————————•———————————

Stansberry Research: Doc... many investors spend a lot of time and energy trying to pick the right stocks. But one's success as a stock picker actually plays a relatively small role when it comes to increasing wealth through investment... much smaller than the average investor realizes.

A much more important aspect to successful investment is called asset allocation. Can you explain what this is, and why it's so important?

Dr. David Eifrig: I'd be happy to. Asset allocation is how you balance your wealth among stocks, bonds, cash, real estate, commodities, and precious metals in your portfolio. This mix is the most important factor in your retirement investing success.

It's 100 times more important than any stock pick. It's 100 times more important than knowing the next hot country to invest in... or what option to buy... or knowing what the housing market is doing... or whether the economy is booming or busting.

I've seen ignorance of this topic ruin more retirements than any other financial factor.

Stansberry Research: How can it ruin a retirement?

Eifrig: Many people have no idea what sensible asset allocation is... So they end up taking huge risks by sticking big chunks of their portfolios into just one or two investments.

For example, I have a friend who had most of her wealth in real estate investments in 2006. When the market busted, she lost a huge portion of her retirement funds.

Or consider employees of big companies that put a huge portion of their retirement money into company stock. Employees of big companies that went bankrupt, like Enron, WorldCom, Bear Stearns, and Lehman Brothers were totally wiped out. They believed in the companies they worked for, so they kept more than half of their retirement portfolios in company stock.

And it's all because they didn't know about proper asset allocation. Because of this ignorance, they lost everything.

I'm sure you can see from these examples that asset allocation is so important because keeping your wealth stored in a good, diversified mix of assets is the key to avoiding catastrophic losses.

If you keep too much wealth – like 80% of it – in a handful of stocks and the stock market goes south, you'll suffer badly. The same goes for any asset... gold, oil, bonds, real estate, or blue-chip stocks. Concentrating your retirement nest egg in just a few different asset classes is way too risky for you. Betting on just one horse is a fool's game.

Stansberry Research: This seems like simple common sense... to spread your risk around.

Eifrig: I agree. But not doing it is an extremely common mistake people make.

Stansberry Research: Could you walk us through what asset classes are out there... and what a sensible mix looks like?

Eifrig: First off, you have one of my favorite assets in the world, which is cash.

"Cash" simply means all the money you have in savings, checking accounts, certificates of deposit (CDs), and U.S. Treasury bills. Anything with less than one year to maturity should be considered cash.

I like to keep plenty of cash on hand so I can be ready to buy bargains in case of a market collapse. Investors flush with cash are often able to get assets on the cheap after a collapse – they can swoop in and pick things up with cash quickly, and often at great prices.

I generally recommend holding between 10% and 45% of your assets in cash, depending on your circumstances. One of the major tenets of good financial planning is to always have at least 12 months of living expenses in cash in case of disaster. **If you haven't started saving yet, this is the No. 1 thing to start today**.

Next, you have conventional stocks. These are investments in individual businesses or investments in a broad baskets of stocks, like mutual funds and exchange-traded funds (ETFs). Stocks are a proven long-term builder of wealth, so almost everyone should own some. But keep in mind, stocks are typically more volatile than most other assets.

Just like you should stay diversified overall with your assets, you should stay diversified in your stock portfolio. I once heard a well-known TV money show host ask callers: "Are you diversified?" According to him, owning five stocks in different sectors makes you diversified. This is simply not true. It is a dangerous notion.

The famous economist Harry Markowitz modeled math, physics, and stock-picking to win a Nobel Prize for the work on diversification. The science showed you need around 12-18 stocks to be fully diversified.

Holding and following that many stocks might seem daunting – it's really not. The problem is easily solved with a mutual fund that holds dozens of stocks, which of course makes you officially diversified.

Stansberry Research: Let's discuss a few more asset categories.

Eifrig: Next you have fixed-income securities, which are generally called "notes" or "bonds." These are basically any instrument that pays out a regular stream of income over a fixed period of time. At the end, you also get your initial investment – which is called your "principal" – back.

Depending on your age and tolerance for risk, bonds sit somewhere between boring and a godsend. The promise of interest payments and an almost certain return of capital at a certain fixed rate for a long period of time always lets me sleep well at night.

Adding safe fixed-income bonds to your portfolio is a simple way to stabilize your investment returns over time. For people with enough capital, locking up extra money (more than 12 months of your expenses) in bonds is a simple way to generate more income than a savings account.

Another asset class is real estate. Everyone knows what this is, so we don't need to spend much time covering this. If you can keep a portion of wealth in a paid-for home, and possibly some income-producing real estate like a rental property or a farm, it's a great diversifier.

Stansberry Research: Do you consider precious metals, like gold and silver, an important piece of a sensible asset allocation?

Eifrig: I do... But gold and silver, to me, are like insurance.

Precious metals like gold and silver typically soar during times of economic turmoil, so I want to own some "just in case."

But I'm different than the standard owner of gold and silver, who almost always believes the world is headed for hell in a hand basket. I'm a major optimist, but I'm also a realist. I believe in owning insurance. I believe in staying "hedged."

For many years, my job at Wall Street bank Goldman Sachs was to develop and implement advanced hedging strategies for wealthy clients and corporations. The goal with these strategies was to protect jobs, wealth, and profits from unforeseen events.

During those years, I learned a big difference between wealthy people and poor people. Wealthy people almost always own plenty of hedges and insurance. They consider what could happen in worst-case scenarios and take steps to protect themselves. Poor people tend to live with "blinders" on.

So just like I wear my seat belt while driving, I own silver and gold – just in case. For most people, most of the time, keeping around 5% of your wealth in gold and silver provides that insurance.

Stansberry Research: That's a great view of gold and silver. So... you've covered five broad categories... cash, stocks, bonds, real estate, and precious metals. Do you have any guidelines on how much of each asset folks should own?

Eifrig: There's no way anyone can provide a "one size fits all" allocation. Everyone's financial situation is different. Asset allocation advice that will work for one person, can be worthless for another.

But most of us have the same basic goals: Wealth preservation... picking up safe income... and safely growing our nest egg. We can all use some guidelines to help make the right individual choices. Keep in mind, what I'm about to say is just a guideline...

If you're having a hard time finding great bargains in stocks and bonds, an allocation of 25%... even 50% in cash is a good idea.

This sounds crazy to some people, but if you can't find great investment bargains, there's nothing wrong with sitting in cash, earning a little interest, and being patient. If great bargains present themselves, like they did in early 2009, you can lower your cash balance and plow it into stocks and bonds.

As for stocks, if you're younger and more comfortable with the volatility involved in stocks, you can keep stock exposure to somewhere between 33% and 50% of your portfolio. A young person who can place a sizable chunk of money into a group of high-quality, dividend-paying stocks and hold them for decades will grow very wealthy.

If you're older and can't stand risk or volatility, consider keeping a huge chunk of your wealth in cash and bonds... like a 75%-85% weighting. Near the end of your career as an investor, you're more concerned with preserving wealth than growing it, so you want to be conservative.

Stansberry Research: Great advice. Any last thoughts?

Eifrig: As you can see from my guidelines, the big thing to keep in mind with asset allocation is that you've got to find a mix that is right for you... that suits your risk tolerance... your station in life.

Whatever mix you choose, just make sure you're not overexposed to an unforeseen crash in one particular asset. This will ensure a long and profitable investment career.

Stansberry Research: Thanks, Doc.

Eifrig: You're welcome.

Learn How to Limit Your Investment Risk Through Intelligent Position Sizing and Stop Losses

Let's say you have the opportunity to buy shares in a great business at a bargain price.

How much should you buy?

If you buy too much, a freak accident with your stock could wipe you out. If you buy too little, you won't take full advantage if things work out well.

This is where "position sizing" and "stop losses" should enter your thinking. They help limit your investment risk… and maximize investment gains.

In the pages that follow, you'll learn all about these essential tools…

How to Master Position Sizing and Stop Losses

An interview with Brian Hunt,
Editor in Chief, Stansberry Research

If you want to succeed as an investor, you need to master two essential tools: Position sizing and stop losses.

In the following interview, Stansberry Research Editor in Chief Brian Hunt explains these tools. Before you buy a single stock or bond, make sure you understand these concepts. They are your greatest protection against an investor's worst nightmare – catastrophic losses.

In the next few pages, you'll learn exactly how to protect your own portfolio with these two very important concepts...

———————————•———————————

Stansberry Research: Brian, one of the most important things any new investor can learn is correct position sizing. Can you define the idea for us?

Brian Hunt: Sure... Position sizing is an incredibly important part of your investment or trading strategy. If you don't know the basics of this concept, it's unlikely you'll ever succeed in the market. Fortunately, it's an easy concept to grasp.

Position sizing is the part of your investment or trading strategy that tells you how much money to place into a given trade.

For example, suppose an investor has a $100,000 account. If this investor buys $1,000 worth of shares in company ABC, his position size would be 1% of his total capital. If the investor buys $3,000 worth of stock, his position size is 3% of his total capital.

Many folks think of position sizing in terms of how many shares they own of a particular stock. But the successful investor thinks in terms of what percentage of their total account is in a particular stock.

Stansberry Research: Why is position sizing so important?

Hunt: Position sizing is the first and probably most important way investors can protect themselves from what's known as the "catastrophic loss."

The catastrophic loss is the kind of loss that erases a large chunk of your investment account. It's the kind of loss that ends careers... and even marriages.

The catastrophic loss typically occurs when a trader or investor takes a much larger position size than he should. He'll find a stock, commodity, or option trade he's really excited about, start dreaming of all the profits he could make, and then make a huge bet.

He'll place 20%, 30%, 40%, or more of his account in that one idea. He'll "swing for the fences" and buy 2,000 shares of a stock instead of a more sensible 300 shares. He'll buy 20 option contracts when he should buy three.

The obvious damage from the catastrophic loss is financial. Maybe that investor who starts with $100,000 suffers a catastrophic 80% loss and is left with $20,000. It takes most folks years to make back that kind of money from their job.

But the less obvious damage is worse than losing money... It's the mental trauma that many people never recover from. They can get knocked out of investing forever. They just stick their money in the bank and stop trying. They consider themselves failures.

They see years of hard work – as represented by the money they accumulated from their job or business – flushed down the toilet. It's a tough "life pill" to swallow. Their confidence gets shattered.

So clearly, you want to avoid the catastrophic loss at all costs... And your first line of defense is to size your positions correctly.

Stansberry Research: What are the guidelines for choosing a position size?

Hunt: Most great investors will tell you to never put more than 4% or 5% of your account into any one position. Some professionals won't put more than 3% in one position. One percent, which is a much lower risk per position, is better for most folks.

Seasoned investors may vary position size depending on the particular investment. For example, when buying a safe, cheap dividend stock, a position size of up to 5% may be suitable.

Some managers who have done a ton of homework on an idea and believe the risk of a significant drop is nearly non-existent will even go as high as 10% or 20% – but that's more risk than the average investor should take on.

When dealing with more volatile vehicles – like speculating on junior resource stocks or trading options – position sizes should be much smaller... like 0.5%... or 1%.

Unfortunately, most novices will risk three, five, or 10 times as much as they should. It's a recipe for disaster if the company or commodity they own suffers a big, unforeseen move... or when the market in general suffers a big unforeseen move. These big, unforeseen moves happen with much greater frequency than most folks realize.

Stansberry Research: Can you explain how the math works with position sizing?

Hunt: Yes... But first I need to explain a concept that goes hand in hand with determining correct position sizing: protective stop losses.

A protective stop loss is a predetermined price at which you will exit a position if it moves against you. It's your "uncle" point where you say, "Well, I'm wrong about this one. Time to cut my losses and move on."

Most people use stop losses that are a certain percentage of their purchase price. For example, if a trader purchases a stock at $10 per share, he could consider using a 10% stop loss. If the stock goes against him, he would exit the position at $9 per share... or 10% lower than his purchase price.

If that same trader uses a stop loss of 25%, he would sell his position if it declined to $7.50 per share, which is 25% less than $10.

Generally speaking, a stop loss of 5% is considered a "tight stop"– close to your purchase price. A 50% stop loss is considered a "wide stop" – a long way from your purchase price.

Combining intelligent position sizing with stop losses will ensure the trader or investor a lifetime of success. To do this, you need to understand the concept many people call "R."

Stansberry Research: Please explain...

Hunt: "R" is the value you will "risk" on any one given investment. It is the foundation of all your position-sizing strategies.

For example, let's return to the example of the investor with a $100,000 account. We'll call him Joe.

Joe believes company ABC is a great investment, and he decides to buy it at $20 per share.

But how many shares should he buy? If he buys too many, he could suffer a catastrophic loss if an accounting scandal strikes the company. If he buys too little, he's not capitalizing on his great idea.

Here's where intelligent position sizing comes into play. Here's where the investor must calculate his R.

R is calculated from two other numbers. One is total account size. In this case, it's $100,000. The other number is the percentage of the total account you'll risk on any given position.

$$R = \text{total account size} \times \% \text{ of account at risk}$$

Let's say Joe decides to risk 1% of his $100,000 account on the position. In this case, his R is $1,000. If he decided to dial-up his risk to 2% of his entire account, his R would be $2,000. If he was a novice or extremely conservative, he might go with 0.5%, or an R of $500.

Joe is going to place a 25% protective stop loss on his ABC position. With these two pieces of information, he can now work backward and determine how many shares he should buy.

Position size =
(100/% stop loss) × R

Remember... Joe's R is $1,000, and he's using a 25% stop loss.

To calculate how large the position will be, the first step is to always divide 100 by his stop loss.

In Joe's case, 100 divided by 25 results in four. Now, he performs the next step in figuring his position size. He takes that number – four – and multiplies it by his R of $1,000.

Four times $1,000 is $4,000, which means Joe can buy $4,000 worth of ABC stock... or 200 shares at $20 per share.

If ABC declines 25%, he'll lose $1,000 – 25% of his $4,000 – and exit the position.

That's it. That's all it takes to practice intelligent position sizing.

Here's the calculation again:

- 100 divided by your stop loss equals "A."

- "A" multiplied by "R" equals position size.

- Finally, position size divided by share price equals the number of shares to buy.

Now... what if Joe wants to use a tighter stop loss – say 10% – on his ABC position? Let's do the math...

- 100 divided by 10 equals 10.

- 10 multiplied by $1,000 equals $10,000.

- $10,000 divided by the same $20 share price equals 500 shares.

So you can see that using a tighter stop loss with the same R allows Joe to buy a larger number of shares, while risking the same amount of his total account... $1,000.

Next, let's say Joe wants to use a super-tight stop loss of just 5% on his position. In this case, if ABC declines just 5% to $19 per share, he's out of the trade.

This tighter stop loss means he can buy even more shares. Let's do the math again...

- 100 divided by 5 equals 20.

- 20 multiplied by $1,000 equals $20,000.

- $20,000 divided by the $20 share price equals 1,000 shares.

Again, a tighter stop loss with the same R of $1,000 means he can buy twice as many shares and still risk the same amount of his total account.

As you can see, you can use the concepts of position sizing and stop losses to determine how much of any asset to buy... from crude-oil futures to currencies to microcaps to Microsoft.

If you're trading a riskier, more volatile asset, the stop-loss percentage should typically increase and the position size should decrease.

If you're investing in a safer, less volatile asset, the stop-loss percentage should decrease and the position size should increase.

And like I mentioned earlier, a good, "middle of the road" R that will work for anyone is 1% of your total account. Folks new to the trading game would be smart to start with 0.5% of their account. This way, you can be wrong 10 times in a row and lose just 5% of your account.

Stansberry Research: Any closing thoughts?

Hunt: Again, the biggest thing intelligent position sizing does is keep you from suffering the catastrophic loss. The golden rule of investing or trading is, "Don't lose money." Intelligent position sizing ensures you always follow rule No. 1.

Stansberry Research: Thanks for talking with us.

Hunt: My pleasure.

— Concept 4 —

Discover the Magic of Compound Interest

Compound interest is the most powerful investment force on the planet. It can either work for you or against you.

Once you get it working for you, you're mathematically guaranteed to grow wealthy.

In this chapter, you'll learn the basics of compound interest – and how to maximize its power.

We'll start with two classic essays in which *Retirement Millionaire* editor Dr. David Eifrig reveals just how powerful the impact of compounding is on your portfolio. In his first example, "Doc" shows you the easiest way to become a millionaire in retirement simply by starting out with $10,000 at the age of 40...

The Easiest Way to Make $1 Million in the Stock Market

By Dr. David Eifrig

By embracing this strategy, you'll be on the road to riches. Ignoring it and getting lazy about using its power means you'll never have a chance for the lifestyle you want.

But first, a warning: You're probably not interested in what Dr. Eifrig has to say. It's not some gold stock that's going to the moon. It's not sexy. It's not a quick fix.

The secret is not hard to grasp. You just have to understand a few simple principles. But as you might imagine, it does take some time and a little effort on your part. And you have to start taking advantage of it right now.

———————•———————

It starts with one simple idea... compound returns.

If you're not sure what compound returns are, don't worry. It's easy to understand and a powerful tool when you put it to work.

Simply stated, compound returns are money you make off the money you make. And the more money you make, the more money your money makes off the money your money makes. I hope you're smiling, but here's what happens...

Imagine you're 40 years old, have a $10,000 investment account, and subscribe to my *Retirement Millionaire* letter. In one year, our portfolio's conservative blend of assets returned a fantastic 18%. If you kept reading year after year and kept making consistent 18% annual returns, what would happen to your portfolio by the time you retire at the age of 68?

You'd have earned a million dollars.

The numbers are simple: If you start investing with $10,000, you'll have about $11,800 (not including taxes or fees) at the end of the first year. You made $1,800 on your initial investment.

But in your second year... you're not starting over at $10,000. The $1,800 you earned in the first year will be making money for you, too.

So assuming gains of 18%, you'll have earned another $1,800 on your original capital plus another $324 on the profits from the previous year's $1,800.

You're not just multiplying $1,800 times 25 years. (That only gives you $45,000.) **The money starts making money on top of itself – your money is compounding**.

The money you make in the first year, in this case $1,800, starts making money in the second year, third year, and so on... It continues this way for every stream of money you compound. So the $1,800 you make in your second year also makes $324 in the third (18% of $1,800).

Take a look at the table below and you'll see that by the end of your third year, you'll have $16,430.

Earning 18% Interest on $10,000

	Year 1	Year 2	Year 3
Total Investment	$10,000	$11, 800	$13,924
18% Interest Earned	$1,800	$2,124	$2,506
Year-End Amount	$11,800	$13,924	$16,430

And the money just keeps building. Take a look at the next chart. You can see how much money you'll have at the end of each year. By age 68 (28 years of compounding), it totals nearly $1 million. And if you wait another couple years, until age 70, the compounding effect starts to explode. At that point, you have almost $1.5 million.

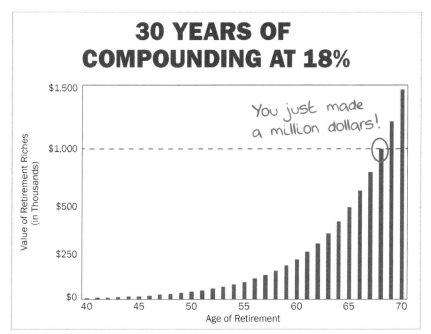

30 YEARS OF COMPOUNDING AT 18%

You just made a million dollars!

You can see why this secret is so powerful. By plowing your earnings back into your portfolio, you can get your money working for itself and amass a fortune from your initial investments.

Retire Early With This Safe Stock System

By Dr. David Eifrig

In his follow-up essay below, Doc explains how you can "super-charge" a successful compounding strategy.

He shares the example of his sister, who became a multi-millionaire in her 50s by simply investing a total of $11,700 – and letting the magic of compounding do the rest...

———————●———————

In the previous essay, I showed you the easiest way to make $1 million in the stock market. It's all about "compound returns"...

As I explained, compound returns are the money you make off the money you make. And the more money you make, the more money your money makes off the money your money makes.

It sounds almost nonsensical... but this idea has incredible power. If you start with a $10,000 portfolio at age 40, you can have more than $1 million by the time you retire.

And it turns out, that's chump change. In this essay, I'll show you the REAL secret to creating wealth through compounding.

This secret is almost as simple as compounding itself. Like compounding, this secret is not "sexy." It's not a hot stock tip. But it can create astounding levels of wealth for investors who follow it. I know because both my father and my sister used it to create a worry-free retirement.

My dad was a fantastic doctor, bright and kind with his patients. But he was a terrible investor. I watched him get greedy (like most people do). I watched him let his losers run and cut his profits off early (like most people do). Occasionally, he'd buy off some tip at a cocktail party (like most people do)...

Luckily, his trading account was just for "play" money, and he rarely paid a lot of attention to it. His retirement account was a different thing. With that money, he took advantage of the one thing that can make anyone wealthy...

My sister did, too. She lives in Bozeman, Montana with her husband and two sons. Their house offers a beautiful view of the mountains. They have the time and money to do most anything they want. I shared today's secret with her decades ago... and she credits me with showing her the way to becoming a millionaire.

You can see the secret in action in this chart:

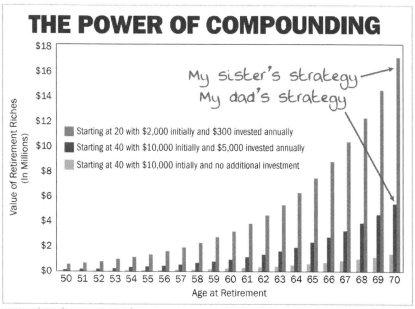

THE POWER OF COMPOUNDING

My sister's strategy
My dad's strategy

Starting at 20 with $2,000 initially and $300 invested annually
Starting at 40 with $10,000 initially and $5,000 invested annually
Starting at 40 with $10,000 intially and no additional investment

Value of Retirement Riches (In Millions)

Age at Retirement

The gray bars represent the strategy I showed you in the previous essay. And it works: $10,000 turns into more than $1 million. But look at the other bars...

The dark blue bars represent my dad's strategy. In my father's case, he started tucking a little bit of money away each year in the retirement plan his university offered for professors. I don't have the exact numbers. But it wasn't as much as the initial amount he used to open the account.

You can see how starting with $10,000 and then just putting in $5,000 a year for the next 20 years makes a person a millionaire by age 60. That's nearly eight years sooner than the plan I showed you previously.

If you continue for just another five years (25 years total), you're a multimillionaire. If you maintain this strategy until age 68, you'll be worth nearly $4 million ($3.862 million to be exact).

Think about this for a minute. You start at age 40, earning what we've been earning in my *Retirement Millionaire* newsletter (18% gains per year) in a balanced and safe mix of securities. You begin with $10,000 and add a little bit more each year ($5,000). And voila... You're a millionaire at age 60.

Now look at the light blue bars, which represent my sister's strategy. What my sister did was apply these same principles in her first job. And she made sure that for every job and raise thereafter, she added a little bit more to the retirement pool.

But for her, it was much easier. She started a lot younger and didn't have to put much in (she didn't have much to put in). The chart shows what happens if, like my sister, you start at age 20 with less than $2,000 and put in just $300 a year after that... You become a millionaire by age 54.

At that point, you've put in a total of $10,200 – and earned $990,000 on the original investments. And if you wait five more years, you become a multimillionaire at age 59. That's a spectacular return on an $11,700 investment plan. (It's 17,000% if you're scoring at home.)

As I showed you with my father's story, you don't need 50 years to appreciate the power of compounding. But as my sister's example proves, the more time you have, the more you can supercharge the power of compounding.

So I suggest you share this "secret" with your friends and family. If you have children or grandchildren, they need to know about savings and investing. One way to teach them is with the story of my sister... how she started with little, added some money every year, and saw it grow to millions of dollars.

The One Phone Number Every Investor Needs to Know

By Dan Ferris
Editor, *Extreme Value*

Dan Ferris, editor of Stansberry Research's *Extreme Value*, is a world-class business analyst and value investor.

His strategy of finding safe, cheap, and profitable stocks has earned him a loyal following – as well as one of the most impressive track records in the industry. *Extreme Value* counts more than 20 major financial firms and well-known fund managers as subscribers.

In this classic educational essay, Dan introduces something called a dividend reinvestment plan (or "DRIP") – a way for your money to earn you more money... and you don't have to lift a finger.

Most people don't know about these plans. But nearly every broker offers them free of charge...

———————●———————

Do you know the one number to call to generate long-term wealth?

I'm not talking about the numbers you see on late-night infomercials for "get rich quick" investment strategies. I'm talking about a single number to dial... and the one short conversation every investor should have.

In five minutes, you can put one of the universe's most powerful forces to work for you. You just need to dial that number.

I did it myself. The number I called was 800-454-9272. That's not necessarily the right number for you. But your number should be easy to find...

Let me explain...

Many online brokers offer an incredible benefit to their clients.

Many of them will – automatically and for free – reinvest the dividends you receive back into the stocks that pay those dividends.

This strategy is called a DRIP – a dividend reinvestment plan. And it's a great way to harness the "king" of all investment ideas: compounding.

By "compounding," I mean making your gains generate more gains.

The key to this strategy is owning a high-quality dividend-raising stock. These "World Dominating Dividend Growers" (or WDDGs) are highly competitive, cash-rich businesses with growing dividends. Investing in these stocks allows you to compound your money at high rates over long periods of time.

We'll use one of my WDDGs, software giant Microsoft (MSFT), as an example...

Let's say you buy 100 shares of Microsoft at $30... And let's assume the share price will grow about 5% a year. You'll collect $80 in dividends in year one.

Now let's say you use those dividends to buy more shares of the stock... and the company continues to raise its dividend like it has since 2005. By year two, you'll collect $92 in dividends... which you can use to buy more stock.

If you keep putting your dividends back into shares of the stock, by year 10, your initial $3,000 investment will be worth $7,595. By year 20, it'll be worth $35,322.

How Much Can You Make From Microsoft?	
Year	Value
0	$3,000
3	$3,817
5	$4,552
10	$7,595
20	**$35,322**

Buying great, dividend-paying companies, holding them for the long term, and reinvesting your dividends is the only sure way I know to safely and easily generate real wealth.

And it's so easy to get started. All you need to do is call your broker. The number I mentioned is for Ameritrade, one of the brokers I use.

It really is that simple. To take advantage of it, all you need to do is call up your broker or send a short e-mail and say, "I'd like to enroll my stock in your free DRIP." (If your broker doesn't offer free dividend reinvesting, seriously consider finding a different broker.)

Using free, automatic dividend reinvesting on high-quality stocks is one of the easiest ways you can start building wealth immediately.

Just pick up the phone.

Realize When It Comes to Buying Stocks, You're Buying Partial Ownership of Real Businesses

Never buy shares of a company that you wouldn't want to own.

When you realize this simple truth, you'll always look to buy high-quality businesses that treat their shareholders well.

This is the secret behind the investment success of legends like Warren Buffett, John Templeton, and Peter Lynch. These money managers made billions of dollars by understanding what makes for a great business.

In the following pages, you'll learn to seek out the attributes of high-quality businesses that smart long-term investors always look to buy. Any investor who hopes to safely make a fortune in stocks cannot afford to ignore these ideas...

What Makes for a Great Business?

An interview with Dan Ferris

Legendary investor Warren Buffett has often said his ideal investment is a wonderful business trading at a fair price.

Many investors are familiar with price-to-earnings ratios, price-to-book values, and other measures of value. But we hear relatively little about what actually makes a great business.

In this interview, Dan discusses the five traits all great businesses share...

———————————●———————————

Stansberry Research: Dan, can you describe what makes a great business?

Dan Ferris: Well, great businesses can be defined a number of ways, but most of them share a few common traits.

One of the most important traits is what's known as a **durable competitive advantage**. Put simply, it's an advantage over the competition that is likely to last for a long time... and often has already lasted for a long time.

In capitalism, when a company is extremely successful, you inevitably get competitors coming in. If a company is making an 80% gross margin, someone will come along and say, "I'm going to undercut them and earn a 70% gross margin." Then someone else comes along and says, "I'm perfectly happy with 60%." Before you know it, it's not 80% anymore... it's 8%.

When a company is able to sustain superior performance over a long period of time, it's a clue there's something special going on... that the company has a tangible advantage in its industry. That's an invaluable trait... and one most of the world's best companies have.

Wal-Mart is so big and efficient, it can do anything any other retailer can do... only much cheaper. ExxonMobil is like that, too. So is UPS. UPS owns an enormous global transportation and logistics network. It's very difficult to compete with.

Burlington Northern and other American railroads have an excellent durable competitive advantage. They own thousands of miles of railroad track, and nobody wants anyone to build more railroad track. Once you get a railroad built through a particular area, chances are folks won't want to allow another to be built there. People don't generally like to have railroads and pipelines in their backyards.

Stansberry Research: A durable competitive advantage. What's another trait?

Ferris: Another important one is **thick profit margins**. A thick profit margin generally indicates a business is efficient at allocating capital and controlling costs, so more of its revenue can be retained as profit. It also means the business has a built-in buffer of safety... meaning the risk that a drop in revenue will cause an operating loss is much lower.

Obviously, this means some industries are much more likely to produce great businesses than others... But if a company can maintain a relatively thick, stable profit margin compared to other businesses in the same industry, it's another big sign you're on to a great business.

Thick profit margins are universally desirable. Everybody in business would much rather net $0.20 in profit for every $1 of sales than $0.02. When you're able to hold off competition AND make a thick profit margin, that's as good a financial result as a business can ever get.

A third characteristic of a great business is **low capital expenditures**. This basically equates to being able to employ a relatively small amount of capital and get incrementally more growth out of it.

A great example here is Microsoft. Microsoft didn't need to build a factory to produce its new Windows operating system. It didn't need to build a mine or buy a million trucks or a million planes or anything of the sort. It required just a small capital investment, next to none really. It might have needed to hire a few more people. Therefore, it is able to make a huge return on its investment. That's a great characteristic.

Warren Buffett often gives the examples of Coca-Cola and See's Candies, because they've required little capital to grow... and they earn so much more than when he first invested in them.

Stansberry Research: Most of the companies you've mentioned are big and super well-known. How important is an elite name brand?

Ferris: A **recognizable brand** that everybody really wants is a big advantage.

Think about the difference between, say, Hershey and any other candy bar...

It's three o'clock in the afternoon, and you feel like having a Hershey bar to get you through the rest of your work day. You walk outside your office, and there's a little store on the corner. You go inside, and see some other brand of chocolate bar, but no Hershey.

Right across the street, there's a 7-Eleven that you know has Hershey bars. I think many, many people would cross the street for the Hershey bar. THAT is a great brand.

When I shave, I use Gillette. There's just no substitute for it. When I sit down for lunch in a restaurant I've never been to, my first question for the server is, "Coke or Pepsi?" If it's Coke, I'm good. If it's Pepsi, I'll have iced tea. At dinner, my first question is, "Do you have Sam Adams?" I hardly ever drink any other beer. I don't think I'm that unusual. People trust certain brands.

That's one of the reasons McDonald's is so successful. You can get exactly the same food at all 30,000 restaurants. It's uncanny when you think about it, how they're able to make all those identical Big Macs all over the world every day.

I could go on, but you get the picture. They could raise the price of Coke, Big Macs, Sam Adams, or Gillette razors by 10% or even 15%, and it wouldn't faze me a bit. That pricing power is one of the primary attributes that makes an elite brand name so valuable as a business.

Of course, it often goes hand in hand with other traits. Coca-Cola is known all over the world. At the same time, it has the world's largest beverage-distribution system... meaning it can sell a lot more of any product than anyone else.

So if you create some new soft-drink product, you can either try to build a distribution system yourself or you can just go to Coke – which has the world's biggest distribution system –

and you could conceivably get that product into more people's hands quicker than by any other means.

Stansberry Research: Any other traits common among great businesses?

Ferris: There's one more that's also related to the others... and that's **scalability**. It's not a coincidence that many of the world's greatest businesses become huge blue-chip companies. A great business can be scaled easily... So given enough time, many of them grow to be large.

It's an advantage in some ways. Obviously, it's a hindrance in others. You can't grow as fast once you're big. But you can still grow. And in general, you can pay for that growth much easier than your smaller competitors can.

Like I mentioned before... Wal-Mart is better at cutting costs and moving large amounts of merchandise for a lower price than anybody else is. ExxonMobil is better at navigating the cycles of the oil and gas industry than anybody else is.

You can go right down the list and say this company is better at this than anybody else is... and it's how it got so enormously big. Wal-Mart, ExxonMobil, Apple, Microsoft... They are some of the biggest companies in the world, and they're all hugely successful.

That's probably the simplest way to see there's something special going on... that they have something other companies don't.

Stansberry Research: Thanks for talking with us, Dan.

Ferris: You're welcome. Take care.

Economic Goodwill

An interview with Porter Stansberry

This idea is not an investment strategy... yet it's the secret behind the success of investment greats like Warren Buffett.

In the following interview, Porter breaks down the idea of "economic goodwill" and how important it is when evaluating a business.

———————————•———————————

Stansberry Research: Economic goodwill is probably one of the least understood ideas in investing. Can you define this idea and explain why it's such an important concept for investors?

Porter Stansberry: Economic goodwill is an accounting term that refers to the intangible assets of a company. It's a simple idea, but a tough subject for most people to get their heads around.

All the excess value of a company – all the stuff that isn't property, equipment, inventory, etc. – goes into the catch-all category of goodwill.

The Securities and Exchange Commission requires companies to write off goodwill over time. The precise rules around goodwill are beyond the scope of this conversation, but there are various tests done against goodwill that the companies then have to appropriately price.

The effect of this is that over time, companies lose the value of their goodwill according to these accounting standards. But in fact, the goodwill of many businesses actually increases over time.

So the bottom line is that the book value of many companies – especially great companies – is often misstated because there isn't enough credit given to the goodwill column.

Stansberry Research: Can you explain why that is?

Stansberry: Sure... let me give you an example.

If you look at the 2014 balance sheet of a company like Coca-Cola, you're going to find a certain amount of value given to goodwill.

But that goodwill – that number on the balance sheet – doesn't compute when you look closely. The company is able to produce enormous returns on net-tangible assets that cannot be explained in the context of free markets. Coke's annual return is something near 90% a year. That doesn't make any sense. That's an unbelievably high return.

It doesn't make any sense because Coke's true net-tangible assets are actually much higher... The true economic goodwill that Coke has is not represented anywhere on its 2014 balance sheet.

So the trick to economic goodwill is to understand there is this invisible asset that can play a huge role in corporate earnings. Coke is able to charge more for carbonated sugar water than the oil companies can charge for gasoline. That doesn't make economic sense, unless you understand the value of its brand... the value of the relationship it has with its customers.

It's the same story for companies like motorcycle manufacturer Harley-Davidson, jewelry chain Tiffany's, candy maker Hershey, etc. These companies that have great relationships with their customers... that have powerful brands... the goodwill that is written out on their balance sheets is totally unrelated to the actual value.

Stansberry Research: How can investors take advantage of this fact?

Stansberry: Because of this discrepancy, these companies can appear to be expensive in the context of normal accounting, but may actually be trading at very low prices. This can be a huge advantage if you know what to look for.

As another example, I recommended Hershey in my newsletter in 2007. At the time, Hershey only had about $500 million of goodwill on its balance sheet.

In comparison, Hershey's total assets were close to $4 billion. It had about $2 billion in current assets, which basically means cash. But what's more important to realize is it only had $250 million of net-tangible assets. It's hard to believe, but it's true, because it also had close to $3.5 billion in debt.

Now, that's not necessarily a bad thing. When you have a stable business like Hershey, it can make good sense to finance your operations with borrowed money.

But the important point is Hershey's net-tangible assets were stated at just $250 million... yet the company makes a billion dollars in cash per year.

This means Hershey's return on net-tangible assets was 400%. That is out of this world... completely off the charts. Had Hershey discovered some secret to earning bigger returns than any company in history, or was something else going on? Of course, the answer was goodwill... It was dramatically undervalued on the balance sheet.

In other words, the most valuable thing it owned was only stated as $500 million, or about 12.5% of its total assets. There's no way Hershey's goodwill was that small.

The truth is, its goodwill was worth more than all of its other assets combined. It was difficult to price exactly what that goodwill was worth, but it was high because the company made so much money.

We can estimate it by thinking about what a reasonable return on net-tangible assets might be. In this case, let's suppose Hershey's true return on net-tangible assets was about 10%. That's a solid return for a company like Hershey.

To get that return, net-tangible assets would actually have been $10 billion rather than the $250 million stated on the balance sheet. This means the company would actually have about $6 billion in "invisible assets" – $10 billion in total assets versus the $4 billion stated on the balance sheet – that didn't show up on the balance sheet.

This means Hershey's goodwill was probably closer to $6 billion than the $500 million we talked about earlier... so it was actually about 10 times higher than stated.

Of course, that's just a simplified example. The point is that companies' balance sheets are often undervalued relative to the real economic value of their goodwill.

In this example, Hershey's true return on net-tangible assets could have been higher or lower. But it's clear that Hershey's goodwill was undervalued on its balance sheet. Because of that, some measures of value will indicate Hershey is more expensive than it actually is.

Stansberry Research: Are there any other clues that a company has much more goodwill than its balance sheet suggests?

Stansberry: Most companies that have a lot of economic goodwill are heavily-branded companies. They're companies with long histories of a consumer love affair, which is probably the best way to describe it.

A great example I mentioned earlier is Harley-Davidson. People who buy Harley-Davidson motorcycles tend to be fanatics. The economic goodwill in that company is generated by the loyalty and the dedication of its customers, and that is really what fuels the returns.

There are companies that aren't strongly branded that have economic goodwill, but they're few and far between.

But again, the best way to uncover these discrepancies in goodwill is to look at the net-tangible assets of a company relative to its cash earnings.

Stansberry Research: Does economic goodwill have any other benefits?

Stansberry: The other great thing about goodwill is that it doesn't require much capital to maintain.

Let's go back to the Hershey example and assume the true value of its goodwill was closer to $6 billion than $500 million.

Well, if it had another $6 billion worth of traditional assets on its balance sheet, it would have to invest a lot of capital to maintain those assets, right? If there are billions more in property, equipment, and inventory, it would require a significant amount of capital to maintain and replenish those assets.

If it had another $5 billion in assets, it might have to spend another billion dollars per year just to maintain it. But if it did that, of course, it wouldn't have *any earnings at all* because it only earned a billion dollars in cash.

So the real value of economic goodwill is that it doesn't cost much to maintain. It's a huge value that is unseen on your balance sheet and doesn't cost you any money to maintain.

This is really, really powerful, especially in the context of inflation because over time, Hershey will be able to raise the price of its chocolate bars in line with inflation. You've seen this happen again and again your entire life.

A Hershey bar used to cost $0.05, then it was $0.10, then it was $0.25, and so on. By mid-2014, it was $1.50. But throughout all that time, Hershey didn't have to spend any more money maintaining its economic goodwill.

It had to spend more money on materials to make chocolate. It had to spend more money on shipping and energy. But it didn't have to spend a penny extra to maintain its economic goodwill. That is why economic goodwill tends to compound at a very high rate over time.

In 2040, Hershey's economic goodwill might be $60 billion instead of $6 billion. And Hershey wouldn't have had to spend any capital to maintain it.

That's a very valuable thing for a company. Instead of having to spend money maintaining that economic goodwill, it can spend it on dividends to shareholders.

That's the real secret behind Warren Buffett's success. He has specialized in investing over the long-term in economic goodwill, and the result speaks for itself.

Stansberry Research: That's a great explanation, Porter. Thanks for talking with us.

Stansberry: You're welcome.

How to Buy the Most Capital-Efficient Stocks, Safely

By Porter Stansberry

In the past couple essays, you've learned how to look at stocks and what makes for a great business. You've learned one of the world's greatest investment secrets: economic goodwill (or as Porter calls it in the next essay, capital efficiency).

So how do you put it all together?

Below, Porter provides a step-by-step guide to making well-informed decisions about buying world-class stocks.

———————•———————

Make sure you save a copy of this essay.

It's a step-by-step, paint-by-numbers guide to making a fortune in stocks. No, I can't promise that your investments will pan out as well as a few of mine have. But anyone is capable of becoming a world-class investor. You only need to do three things...

1) Find companies that will last.

2) Only buy capital-efficient stocks that offer the potential of compounding returns.

3) Buy shares at "no-risk" prices.

This represents a career of thinking and writing about investments. This is hard-won wisdom. **These are the things I know work – no matter what else is happening in the world or in the markets**.

Investing is a simple game.

The goal is to get the most in return for having given the least in exchange. Any serious study of this process will reveal that just a few variables control the outcome.

First, the amount of capital employed is important. Thus, the cardinal rule is: *Don't lose money.* Money lost cannot be invested. Money lost will not compound.

Second, time matters. The duration an investment may be held continuously with dividends reinvested is critical.

And the third important factor is the rate of compound growth.

What's funny about this list is how simple the game really is... and how few people pay any attention to the most basic rules. I doubt many investors consider these variables before they buy a stock. What most people consider is simply, "Will this stock go up? By how much? And when should I sell?"

The questions they should be asking are almost the complete opposite.

They should try to figure out...

1) How fast are these shares likely to compound, assuming I reinvest all the dividends?

2) How long will I be able to safely hold this company?

3) And most important, what's the most I can safely pay for this stock?

There's one sure way to get rich. And that is to buy capital-efficient businesses (another term for businesses with lots of economic goodwill) that have long-lived products and are capable of increasing payouts year after year.

This approach is, without question, the best way to invest. It's exactly the approach master investor Warren Buffett uses. But it's difficult to explain. Worst of all... once you understand how it works, it's just too simple. All you have to do is buy the kind of companies that excel at returning capital to their owners (the shareholders). Then you reinvest that capital. Rinse and repeat. It's not much harder than washing your hair.

And that means it's boring. For publishers, boring is the kiss of death. So please... forgive me. But the truth is, **using this kind of a strategy over time will produce returns that dwarf the gains you're likely to make speculating, even if you're a great speculator**.

Best of all, my approach, which is based on *capital efficiency*, is totally safe and requires almost zero effort. The whole trick lies in understanding which companies are capital-efficient and have good long-term prospects. Once you know that... you only buy when you can get the shares at such a low price that they essentially carry no risk.

These situations develop all the time. Let me show you this approach as it was implemented in real time, during one of the worst periods in the history of the stock market...

One of the Greatest Investments of My Career

Again, I first recommended shares of Hershey (HSY) back in December 2007 – calling it "Our Best No-Risk Opportunity Ever."

At the time, the stock was trading for around $40. By the end of 2008 – after a huge bear market where the average stock fell by 50% – Hershey's shares had hardly budged. The stock was trading around $35. We weren't stopped out.

By December 2009, two years after our original recommendation, the shares still hadn't budged. The stock was still trading for around $40. Subscribers were irate. "When is this dog going to move higher?" they asked.

Meanwhile, I knew that sooner or later, the shares would take off. I was convinced this stock would be one of the greatest investments of my career.

And from January 2010 to February 2014, Hershey trended higher. In that time, the share price went up 220%, versus the S&P 500's 70% return. And it continued to increase its dividends. What did I see that the market missed?

Between 2005 and early 2014, Hershey had repurchased more than $1 billion worth of its own stock – more than 10% of the company, in addition to paying large ($200 million-plus) cash dividends. It had paid 325 quarterly dividends in a row – 81 years. It had increased its dividend payout every year since 1974.

On a combined basis (dividends and buybacks), the company paid out a remarkably large amount of the cash it produced. For example... in 2008, the company produced a little more than $500 million in cash from operations. It spent nearly $300 million on dividends and share buybacks. (It also repaid $128 million in debt.)

Hershey could afford to return so much capital to its shareholders because it required little capital to grow. Since the late-1990s, the company's annual capital spending had remained essentially unchanged. In 1997, the firm invested $172 million in property and equipment.

By the end of 2010, its annual capital budget had only increased to $179 million – essentially unchanged. Meanwhile, cash profits had reached nearly $1 billion – growth of nearly 200%.

This is the beauty of a capital-efficient business: While sales and profits grow, capital investments don't.

And that leads to the real secret – the most important investment secret you will ever be told. Some companies, like Hershey, can increase the percentage of the earnings they pay out as they grow. Let me make sure you understand this...

The size of the payout Hershey makes to investors doesn't merely increase on a nominal basis along with sales... It increases as a percentage of the company's gross profits.

These payouts aren't linear. You have to be willing to wait five or 10 years to appreciate what the company is capable of paying out. For example, during the financial crisis of 2008 and 2009, Hershey's management retained capital to guarantee its competitive and financial position.

It's these payouts – which return cash to shareholders and increase the value of the stock by reducing the size of the float – that are the key to understanding the predictions I made when I first recommended the stock.

Here's what I wrote...

> Let's assume that, thanks to share-count reduction, sales growth, and the company's incredible capital efficiency, it is able to increase the total amount of capital it returns to shareholders each year by 15%. The company currently pays out about $500 million per year, on average, to shareholders. Ten years from now, growing that payout at 15% per year, it should pay out almost $1.7 billion annually.

Today, the stock has a blended yield (cash dividend plus buyback) of about 5.5%. Assuming the yield falls in the future to, say, 3.5% as investors begin to appreciate the value of the company, the shares will be worth $50 billion. Today, the total market value of all of the shares outstanding is a little more than $8 billion. Today's investor would make 525% in capital gains in 10 years, assuming he didn't reinvest the cash dividends (which would increase the return).

Lest you think my 15% growth rate number is too high, I generated it by comparing the actual annual increase in free cash flow per share from 1999 through 2007, which has been a little more than 15% annually. This number is tightly correlated to dividend and buyback amounts because it's the amount of money the company earns after all capital expenses have been paid and it reflects the compounding effect of the company's share repurchases.

Here's the part that's hard to get your head around... Thanks to the miracle of compounding, if this rate of growth continues over 20 years, investors should expect to make 20 times their money or capital gains in excess of 1,900%. Again, that's not including the impact of reinvesting the cash dividends, which would significantly increase returns.

There aren't many businesses that you can realistically expect to make you 20 times your money. There are even fewer businesses that you can expect to hold safely for 20 years. But in this case, you can. This company's leading product has remained totally unchanged for more than 100 years.

Hershey has all the qualities you want in a real, long-term investment – which is why I've spent so much time going over the recommendation again with you. Hershey may be the best long-term investment in the world because it will never be sold to another company. This last point is vastly underappreciated by most investors...

I can't tell you how many times a great business I've owned or recommended has been purchased for a price that excited investors (because of a big short-term gain), but was bitterly disappointing for me because it meant our gains would no longer compound.

A great example was when InBev purchased Anheuser-Busch in 2008. Most subscribers cheered because we got $70 in cash for a stock we'd bought in the $40s. But I mourned the loss of a company I knew I would have never sold.

And that, to me, is the best thing about Hershey. It has a controlling shareholder – The Hershey Trust Company – that's literally not allowed to sell. Ever. Milton Hershey established the trust to benefit the Milton Hershey School, which he created for disadvantaged children. The school educates underprivileged children and pays for their entire education, all the way through college.

Back in 2002, after listening to a bunch of investment bankers who were eager for deal fees, the trust decided it needed to "diversify" its endowment beyond the shares of only one stock, Hershey Co.

When you've got a business this good, anything else you buy is bound to be a disappointment. Clearly, the folks running the trust were about to make a big mistake.

Luckily, the decision to sell so enraged the public in Pennsylvania, the state legislature passed a law requiring the trust to give advanced notice of any sale or merger that would result in the Hershey Trust no longer having complete voting control over Hershey Co. The law further provides specific authority for the attorney general to stop any transaction that isn't necessary to the future economic viability of Hershey Co.

If you're a long-term investor who's looking to cash in over many years by reinvesting dividends and watching your investment compound, having a controlling shareholder that's not allowed to sell is the perfect setup. The trust isn't allowed to sell, so it must focus exclusively on improving the results of Hershey – and increasing the payouts.

There's one other consideration... **How much should you pay for a stock like this or any other long-term investment?** This ends up being the most important variable because the first rule of investing is *don't lose money*. Remember... money you lose doesn't compound.

Here's an easy rule of thumb to use when trying to figure out a safe price to pay for a stock. Just figure out how much money it would take to buy back every share at

the current market price and add in the total net debt of the company. The number you'll end up with is called *enterprise value*. That's the figure it would cost (in theory) for the company to buy itself.

Next, just figure out if there's any realistic way the company could afford to buy itself. Few companies actually go private this way... But bear with me. In 2014, Hershey's enterprise value was $15 billion.

For the company to borrow this much money, it would have had to afford roughly $1 billion a year in interest payments (assuming 7% interest). That's more than its operating income at the time... which means Hershey couldn't afford to buy itself.

On the other hand... when we first recommended the stock, its shares were about 50% cheaper, which put its enterprise value down around $10 billion. Doing the same calculation leaves you with an annual interest bill of around $700 million – something that was just inside the range of possibility back in 2009, when the company earned $769 million from operations.

This kind of analysis shows whether a company could realistically repay all of its debts and all of its shares. Assuming it can afford to do both, there's no fundamental difference between the risk of its stock and the risk of its bonds – because all the bonds and shares could be repurchased.

And that means on a fundamental basis, you're getting all the upside of the shares – all the upside of being an owner – with the same low risk of being a creditor. I call this buying at a "no-risk" price. There's no additional risk to buying the equity compared with the debt.

This is the best analysis to consider before you buy any stock – but especially one you're buying to hold for the long term. You have to make sure you will be comfortable enough to wait for the payoff. You have to make sure you've bought at a good, safe price.

In this case, you'd have a situation where you are extremely unlikely to lose money that should compound at about 15% per year over the long term and that you are extremely unlikely to ever have to sell. That's exactly the kind of situation you should be looking for, all the time.

❧ It's the Best Way to Get Rich

Most people think Warren Buffett became the richest investor in history – and one of the richest men in the world – because he bought the right "cheap" stocks. And legions of professional investors tell their clients they're "Dodd and Graham value investors… just like Warren Buffett." The truth of the matter is entirely different.

Until 1969, Buffett was a value investor, in the style of David Dodd and Benjamin Graham. That is, he bought stocks with stock market capitalizations that were a fraction of their net assets. Buffett figured buying $1 bills for $0.25 wasn't a bad business. And it's not.

But it's not nearly as great of a business as investing in safe stocks that can compound their earnings *for decades*. Take shares of Coca-Cola, for example – they're the best example of Buffett's approach. Like my Hershey example, Buffett's Coke investment was based on capital efficiency.

Buffett bought his Coke stake between 1987 and 1989. It was a huge investment for him at the time, taking up about 60% of his portfolio. How could Buffett have known Coke would be a safe stock… and that it would turn into a great investment?

Well, like Einstein famously said about God, Buffett didn't roll dice. He only bought sure things. He knew Coke's business was incredibly capital-efficient. And judging by its previous marketing results and its expansion into new markets, its sales would also continue growing. As Buffett would tell you, it wasn't that hard to figure out.

Later, other investors would bid up the shares to stupid levels. Coke was trading for more than 50 times earnings by 1998, for example. But Buffett never sold. It didn't matter to him how overvalued the shares were, as long as the company kept raising the dividend.

In 2011, Coke paid out $1.88 in dividends per share. Adjusted for splits and dividends already paid, Buffett paid $3.75 per share for his stock in 1988. Coke's annual dividend equaled 50% of Buffett's total purchase price. Each year, he earns 50% of that investment – whether the stock goes up or down.

In his 1993 letter to Berkshire Hathaway shareholders, Buffett wrote about his Coke investment and his approach – buying stable, capital-efficient companies with the intention of holding them forever so their compounding returns would make a fortune. Here's an excerpt...

> At Berkshire, we have no view of the future that dictates what businesses or industries we will enter. Indeed, we think it's usually poison for a corporate giant's shareholders if it embarks upon new ventures pursuant to some grand vision. We prefer instead to focus on the economic characteristics of businesses that we wish to own...
>
> Is it really so difficult to conclude that Coca-Cola and Gillette possess far less business risk over the long term than, say, any computer company or retailer? Worldwide, Coke sells about 44% of all soft drinks, and Gillette has more than a 60% share (in value) of the blade market.
>
> Leaving aside chewing gum, in which Wrigley is dominant, I know of no other significant businesses in which the leading company has long enjoyed such global power... The might of their brand names, the attributes of their products, and the strength of their distribution systems give them an enormous competitive advantage, setting up a protective moat around their economic castles.

Buffett looks for companies that produce high annual returns when measured against the company's asset base and require little additional capital. He looks for a kind of financial magic – *companies that can earn excess returns without requiring excess capital*. He looks for companies that seem to grow richer every year without demanding continuing investment.

In short, the secret to Buffett's approach is buying companies that produce huge returns on tangible assets without large annual capital expenditures. He calls this attribute "economic goodwill." I call it "capital efficiency."

These kinds of returns shouldn't be possible in a rational, free market. Fortunately, people are not rational. They frequently pay absurdly high retail prices for products and services they love. Buffett explained how another of his holdings, See's Candy, earned such high rates of return on its capital in his

<u>1983 annual letter</u>, which I urge everyone to read. In explaining See's ability to consistently earn a high return on its assets (25% annually, without any leverage), Buffett wrote...

> It was a combination of intangible assets, particularly a pervasive favorable reputation with consumers based upon countless pleasant experiences they have had with both product and personnel. Such a reputation creates a consumer franchise that allows the value of the product to the purchaser, rather than its production cost, to be the major determinant of selling price...

That's the whole magic. When a company can maintain its prices and profit margins because of the value placed on its product by the purchaser rather than its production cost... that business that can produce excess returns – returns that aren't explainable by rational economics. And those, my friend, are exactly the kinds of companies you want to own.

And... *you especially want to own these stocks during inflationary periods.* As things get more and more expensive, capital-efficient companies will have to buy less of them than other companies, on average. The result will be that inflation tends to lift their profits, rather than reduce them.

Now... if it were that simple, we'd all be rich. Buying these kinds of stocks is actually extremely difficult because you rarely get the opportunity to buy them at reasonable prices, let alone no-risk prices.

That's why I urge you to make a list of these kinds of companies... to determine the price at which you can buy them on a no-risk basis... and then wait for your opportunity.

Strive to buy the companies whose products and services you believe are most loved and most likely to be extremely long-lived. Try to acquire assets that your children's children will never want to sell. Set your family's wealth on the path of compounding. In time, you can join the Rockefellers – but only if you never sell.

Learn That the Most Important Aspect of Any Investment Is the Price You Pay

In Concept 5, you learned how to identify great businesses... but that's only half the battle...

No matter how great a business is, it can still be a poor investment if you pay too much. World-class investors don't just focus on buying great businesses. They also focus on buying them at the right prices.

In the following interview, you'll learn why the price you pay is "the most important aspect of any investment"...

The Most Important Aspect of Any Investment

An interview with Brian Hunt

If you want to be successful in stocks, there's one simple thing you have to do: Focus on the price you pay.

You need to buy at bargain prices.

It sounds simple. But most people can't bring themselves to do it.

In the below interview, Stansberry Research Editor in Chief Brian Hunt explains this vital idea... and how you can use it to make winning investments.

———————•———————

Stansberry Research: Brian, at Stansberry Research, we urge people to focus on the price they pay for investments. Could you explain why this is so important?

Brian Hunt: Sure.

This whole idea comes down to treating your investments like you treat almost anything else you buy. The idea is that you should focus on finding good values... and not overpaying for things.

When you buy a pair of shoes, you want to pay a good price. When you buy a computer, you want to pay a good price. When you buy a house, you want to pay a good price. You don't want to overpay. You don't want to embarrass yourself by getting ripped off.

Yet... when people invest, the idea of paying a good price is often cast aside. They get excited about a story they read in a magazine... or how much their brother-in-law is making in a stock, and they just buy it. They don't pay any attention to the price they're paying... or the value they're getting for their investment dollar.

Warren Buffett often repeats a valuable quote from investment legend Ben Graham: *"Price is what you pay, value is what you get."*

That's a great way to put it.

Stansberry Research: How about an example of how this works?

Hunt: Like many investment concepts, it's helpful to think of it in terms of real estate...

Let's say there's a great house in your neighborhood. It's an attractive house with solid, modern construction and new appliances. It could bring in $30,000 per year in rent. This is the "gross" rental income... or the income you have before subtracting expenses.

If you could buy this house for just $120,000, it would be a good deal. Since $30,000 goes into $120,000 four times, you could get back your purchase price in gross rental income in just four years. In this example, we'd say you're paying "four times gross rental income."

Now... let's say you pay $600,000 for that house. Since $30,000 goes into $600,000 a total of 20 times, you would get back your purchase price in gross rental income in 20 years. In this example, we'd say you're paying "20 times gross rental income." Paying $600,000 is obviously not as good a deal as paying just $120,000.

Remember, in this example, we're talking about buying the same house. We're talking about the same amount of rental income.

In one case, you're paying a good price. You're getting a good deal. You'll recoup your investment in gross rental income in just four years.

In the other case, you're paying a lot more. You're not getting a good deal. It will take you 20 years just to recoup your investment. And it's all a factor of the price you pay.

Stansberry Research: Let's move on to a stock market example.

Hunt: Sure. It works the same way.

Let's say Company ABC generated $1 million in annual profit last year.

If you buy ABC at a market value of $6 million, you're paying six times earnings. If you buy ABC at a market value of $20 million, you're paying 20 times earnings. If you buy ABC for a market value of $50 million, you're paying 50 times earnings.

The market is made up of people. And people tend to act crazy from time to time. One month, the market might set the price of ABC at $6 million. The next month, it might set the price of ABC at $8 million or $10 million.

I know that sounds like a wide range of prices, but you see these ranges in the stock market all the time. People are willing to pay different prices for different businesses at different times.

The amount people are willing to pay for a company's earnings is often called the "price-to-earnings multiple," or simply "the multiple."

In this example, it's a much, much better deal to buy shares of ABC when the market is valuing it at $6 million – or at a multiple of six – instead of buying shares when it is valued at $50 million – or a multiple of 50. You get more value for your investment dollar. You're buying shares in a cash-producing enterprise for a lot less.

The job of the investor is to make sure to buy assets at reasonable prices... and avoid buying assets at bloated, expensive prices.

Stansberry Research: If you're buying a great business, does it really matter if you pay too much?

Hunt: It's vitally important to know that buying shares in a great business can turn out to be a terrible investment if you pay the wrong price.

Let's go back to ABC. Let's say it's a great company. It has a good brand and good profit margins. It's steadily growing. And remember, it does $1 million in annual profit.

If you purchase ABC shares at a market value of $100 million, that's paying 100 times earnings for ABC. This is an extremely expensive price. Your only shot at making money in this example is if someone else comes along and is willing to pay an even crazier price than you did.

While this "waiting for a greater fool" can work occasionally, it's generally a losing strategy. The regular investor will never be able to make it work.

What often happens is that the company keeps doing well, but the multiple people are willing to pay returns to more normal levels. In a case like this, the company can keep increasing its profits, but the share price will plummet. It can fall 50% or 75%.

I know this sounds extreme, but it's exactly what happened during and after the 1999 and 2000 market peak.

Back then, good companies with solid future prospects – like Wal-Mart and Microsoft – traded for 50, 60, even 90 times earnings. People who purchased shares back then paid stupid prices. They had speculative fever. They didn't focus on getting good value for their investment dollars.

Because many stocks with good business models were so overvalued, their share prices crashed and went nowhere for many years.

Keep in mind, the underlying businesses were still sound. Those businesses were still growing. But the stock prices got so out of whack, investors who overpaid suffered horribly. It took a long time for the stocks to "work off" their extremely overvalued state.

For example, in 1999, Wal-Mart traded for more than 50 times earnings. It spent more than a decade working off that overvaluation. Folks who bought Wal-Mart back in 1999 didn't make any money for more than a decade. The company did fine... But shareholders who bought the stock at stupid prices suffered for a long time.

If you can buy a great business for 10 times earnings, it's a good deal. But if you pay 30 or 50 times earnings for it, you're bound to be disappointed.

I have to state it again: **If you overpay, you can make a horrible investment in a great company**.

Stansberry Research: On the other hand, you can make money in a poor business if you pay a bargain price, right?

Hunt: Yes. Let's look at another example...

Let's say Company XYZ is barely profitable with a market value of $2 million. It makes just $250,000 a year. And a competitor is doing a better job of serving customers... so sales are declining.

But let's also say that the company sits on a valuable piece of real estate, which it owns free and clear. You know the piece of property could easily sell for $3 million... maybe even $4 million.

You could buy up shares, knowing full well the business is in decline and could even stop being a profitable enterprise. But if you buy shares while the market values the company at $2 million, you could make a great profit if they close the business and sell the assets for at least $3 million.

In this example, you could make money in a bad business... by paying a bargain price. Again, it all comes down to the price you pay.

Stansberry Research: What if you're buying a stock to collect dividends? How do you know what a good price is?

Hunt: The price you pay for a dividend-producing stock is a huge deal.

Let's say Company ABC is a great business that pays a stable dividend. It has raised its dividend every year for 29 consecutive years. Its current annual dividend is $1 per share.

If you bought ABC at $20 per share, your dividend yield would be 5%. If you bought ABC at $30 per share, your dividend yield would be 3.3%. If you bought ABC at $36 per share, your dividend yield would be 2.8%. If you bought ABC at $100 per share, your dividend yield would be just 1%.

As the price you pay goes up, the yield on your original investment goes down.

Obviously, you want to pay lower prices and earn higher yields.

It's a similar story with bonds. Bonds pay fixed-income payments. But like stocks, the prices of bonds can fluctuate.

For example, let's say we have a bond that is issued at a price of $1,000. Let's say it pays a 5% interest rate. That's $50 in annual interest.

If investors lose faith in the company that issues the bond, the bond price could fall to $700. But the annual interest payment would remain $50.

In this case, the buyer of the bond who pays $700 would earn about 7% in annual interest. The difference in how much income you earn is all a function of the price you pay.

Stansberry Research: Any parting thoughts?

Hunt: The big takeaway here is that investors need to view their stock, bond, real estate, and commodity purchases just like they would view buying a house or a car or a phone or their groceries. Don't be a sucker and overpay. Make sure you get good value for your investment dollar. Hunt for bargains.

You wouldn't pay $50 for a gallon of milk, would you? So why would you pay absurd prices for stocks?

Before you buy an asset, study its valuation history. See what levels represent "good prices" and see what levels represent "stupid" prices. These prices vary from stock to stock and asset class to asset class. Make sure you buy at levels that represent historical bargains.

Stansberry Research: Great points. Thank you.

Hunt: You're welcome.

Summary: Investors need to view their stock, bond, real estate, and commodities purchases just like they would view buying a car, phone, or groceries – don't overpay. Even buying a great company at a "stupid" price can make for a terrible investment. Make sure you're getting a good value for your investment dollar by buying an asset at a good historical valuation.

Realize Popular Investments Are Almost Always a Bad Deal... And Unpopular Investments Are Often Incredible Bargains

Asset classes like stocks, commodities, bonds, and real estate go through cycles. They go through periods of being very popular and being very unpopular.

When an asset is popular, lots of people want to buy it. When lots of people want to buy something... they bid the price up, and it becomes a terrible bargain.

When an asset is unpopular... the price declines, and it can become a great bargain.

You want to buy great values, not terrible bargains.

In this chapter, you'll learn about judging investor sentiment and how to find great bargains in unexpected places...

Judging Investor Sentiment

An interview with Dr. Steve Sjuggerud
Editor, *True Wealth*

This idea is a favorite of legendary investors like Warren Buffett and Jim Rogers, yet it's simple enough for a third grader to understand.

Dr. Steve Sjuggerud – editor of Stansberry Research's *True Wealth* service and a master investor – has had tremendous success with this idea. He has used it for years to help make huge, safe returns for tens of thousands of his subscribers.

Read on to discover how you can begin to put it to use in your own investing. This interview is brief, but it could be one of the most valuable lessons you'll read...

———————●———————

Stansberry Research: Steve, in your 20-year career as an investor and newsletter advisor, you've made a lot of spectacular market calls and recommendations. And you've used the idea of judging investor sentiment to help you make those calls.

Can you define this idea... and discuss how people can use it to make safe investments?

Steve Sjuggerud: Absolutely. Using sentiment to find great investment opportunities comes down to going against what the majority of investors are doing. The key to using it correctly is knowing that sentiment only works at the real extremes...

When no one can stand the thought of owning a particular kind of investment, chances are good that it's time to buy. A great example of this situation was stocks in early 2009. Most people were selling their stocks and completely disinterested in buying more... But it was actually a fantastic time to buy. I personally borrowed money to buy stocks around that time – the only time I've done that in my entire career.

On the other hand, when everyone loves an asset – like when everyone loved tech stocks in 2000 – chances are good that the asset is expensive, dangerous, and due for a big fall.

Stansberry Research: Why is that the case?

Sjuggerud: It's just human nature. Most folks like to be with the crowd... That's what feels comfortable.

Most investors – even professional investors like mutual-fund managers – would rather make investments that everyone else is making because that's what makes them feel comfortable and safe. Actually focusing on the value they are getting for their investment dollar is often a secondary consideration.

The trouble is, by the time everyone likes a particular investment, the big gains are already gone. It's going to be overvalued. And ironically, it's often going to be dangerous.

By the time everyone jumped into stocks in 2000, it was too late to make big gains. By the time everyone jumped into real estate in 2006, it was too late to make big gains. In both cases, the markets became horribly overpriced and eventually crashed.

Stansberry Research: So what tools can we use to measure investor sentiment?

Sjuggerud: Judging investor sentiment is just as much an "art" as it is a "science." You have to learn how to recognize extremes in investor sentiment.

Stansberry Research: Can you describe some of the ways that you gauge investor sentiment?

Sjuggerud: There's a big list of indicators that I follow... There are lots of statistical studies of investor sentiment. I've even crunched a lot of numbers myself with expensive computer programs and data sets.

I monitor surveys of individual investors, surveys of money managers, and surveys of what newsletter advisors are saying. I also watch how much money is flowing into particular investment funds, where big hedge funds are positioned in the futures markets, and I monitor a few economic surveys... like consumer sentiment.

Each one measures a different aspect of investor sentiment... and I don't place any single one above all the others. It's about following them all, and taking the weight of the evidence into account.

My friend Jason Goepfert does a great job of monitoring many of these indicators with his SentimenTrader website, and I highly recommend his service as a "one-stop shop" for keeping a tab on investor sentiment. It's what I use.

Again, the key here is to look for situations of extreme pessimism or extreme optimism. When everyone thinks the same thing, everyone is probably wrong. The extremes are what's important.

You have to be on the lookout for situations where everyone in the room is bullish on something or bearish on something. **If everyone is bullish on something, I'm going to avoid it. If everyone is bearish on something, I'm probably going to buy it**.

One of the smartest things super-investor Warren Buffett ever said was that *"you want to be fearful when others are greedy, and greedy when others are fearful."*

Stansberry Research: How do you use sentiment to invest? Do you immediately buy something just because it's hated or unloved?

Sjuggerud: No, and that's an important point...

I do love using sentiment as part of my trading "edge." I love that you can't easily measure "cocktail party chatter" with an index or a computer. But just because an asset is hated or unloved or ignored isn't enough of a reason to buy. I also like to make sure a given asset has stopped falling in price, and is starting to show a bit of an uptrend before I commit my money.

Waiting on a bit of an uptrend ensures the market is starting to recognize the opportunity I see. Waiting on the uptrend ensures I'm not sitting on "dead money," where the asset moves sideways in price for years. Hated assets can move sideways for a decade or more, especially after a huge crash like we had in tech stocks and real estate.

My recipe for making hundreds of percent gains in an investment is finding an asset that is hated or ignored, trading for a cheap price, and just starting an uptrend.

By sticking with this formula, I've been able to make big investment gains without taking much risk.

Stansberry Research: Thanks for talking with us, Steve.

Sjuggerud: You're welcome.

Learn to Appreciate a Good Crisis

An interview with Brian Hunt

The following interview details one of the world's best investment strategies…

It's a strategy used by elite investors like Warren Buffett and Jim Rogers to buy extremely cheap assets.

This strategy involves an unconventional way of looking at world events. And once you adopt this mindset, it will put you ahead of 99% of your fellow investors. In the interview below, Stansberry Research Editor in Chief Brian Hunt discusses what differentiates a master investor from an amateur…

———————●———————

Stansberry Research: You say master investors and traders are often marked by their unconventional view of crisis situations.

Can you describe this view… and why it is part of the master investor's mindset?

Brian Hunt: Sure. I believe a trait great traders and investors almost always possess is the ability to appreciate a good crisis.

A great investor sees crisis situations for what they usually are… tremendous opportunities. They are opportunities to buy assets at cheap, depressed prices… and then earn large gains later.

When a great investor reads a headline like *"European stock markets crash"* or *"Offshore drilling stocks plummet in wake of Gulf of Mexico oil spill,"* he perks up. He starts wondering if the crisis has created investment bargains.

Most investors don't realize this, but a crisis situation is one of the few times you'll ever get to buy assets for bargain prices. A crisis creates panic. When people panic, they dump stocks and bonds and commodities with little regard to their real values. They just sell first and ask questions later.

This air of irrationality creates irrational asset prices. If you can keep your cool, you can take advantage of the irrationality and buy assets on the cheap. This leads to huge gains down the road.

Great investors run toward a crisis. Amateur investors run away from a crisis.

Stansberry Research: Discuss the amateur mindset.

Hunt: The amateur investor – the guy who always struggles in the market – sees crisis situations much, much differently than the master.

He'll read those same headlines: *"European stock markets crash"* and *"Offshore drilling stocks plummet in wake of Gulf of Mexico oil spill,"* and think to himself, "Wow... that news is bad. I'm glad I don't own those stocks."

Or if he is an owner of those stocks, he panics and sells them. He reacts to the news... not the values.

The amateur investor is almost always focused on buying whatever the most popular story is at the time. He's focused on doing what everyone else is doing. He seeks the comfort of the crowd. You can't blame him. Huddling with the crowd is how humans survived 50,000 years ago. You were either part of the tribe or you would die. But in the investment market, it's a recipe for disaster.

Seeking the comfort of the crowd... buying what's popular... buying what is enjoying rosy headlines leads people to buy expensive, overpriced assets.

The master doesn't like to buy overpriced assets. He prefers to buy bargains.

Stansberry Research: What are some examples of a crisis creating trading and investing opportunities?

Hunt: The Gulf of Mexico oil spill during the summer of 2010 is a good example.

That oil spill was one of the worst accidents in the history of the American oil business. It released huge amounts of oil into the ocean. The early efforts to cap the well failed, which made the crisis drag on and on. It was on the news all day every day for over a week.

In response, offshore-drilling stocks of all kinds were crushed. Even good companies that had nothing to do with the oil spill fell over 33%. Transocean, the company involved in the accident, fell about 50%.

Good drilling businesses were sold down to valuations of around five times earnings. That's a cheap price for them... and it was created by a crisis.

After the selloff, I went long offshore drilling stocks and made a big return in a short amount of time. Most of the offshore drillers rebounded at least 25% in just a few months.

Another example is the European debt crisis of 2012. Back then, everyone was worried that the European banks would explode. They were worried governments would default on their debts. They were worried about a European depression. It was all over the news constantly.

In response, European stock markets crashed. Spain's version of the Dow Industrials Average fell from 8,500 to 6,000 in just a few months. That's a 29% crash. Most other European stock markets crashed as well.

If an investor stepped in amidst all that crisis and pessimism and bought European stocks, he made great returns over the next year. The Spanish stock market gained 66% off its bottom in just 15 months. The Greek stock market doubled off its bottom in less than a year.

The 1998 Russian debt crisis was much bigger than the 2012 European crisis. Back then, people thought Russia itself was going to implode. The government defaulted on its debt, and the currency collapsed. The Russian stock market hit a low in late 1998. Ten years later, it had gained more than 6,000%. That's a six with a thousand after it.

Investing during a crisis can produce truly spectacular returns.

Stansberry Research: How about the U.S. credit crisis of 2008? That's what comes to mind when most people hear "crisis."

Hunt: The wake of the 2008 credit crisis was a fantastic time to invest and trade.

This period was marked by the bankruptcy of Lehman Brothers, which was the largest corporate bankruptcy in U.S. history. The housing market crashed. The stock market fell 39% in 2008, which was its worst year since the Great Depression. We were on the verge of a global economic meltdown.

But the world has a funny way of not ending. It turned out that late 2008 and early 2009 were great times to buy elite businesses like Apple, Altria, and Starbucks. Apple tripled in value off its 2009 bottom in less than two years. Altria doubled off its bottom in about two years. Starbucks more than tripled in value off its bottom in about two years.

Commercial real estate, as measured by the large commercial investment fund iShares Real Estate, also more than doubled off its bottom in just two years. One of the top mining firms in the world, Freeport-McMoRan, more than tripled off its bottom.

All those assets were deeply depressed because of the mass selling... because of the pessimism. The crisis created bargains. Everything was so depressed and cheap, it was like a coiled spring. When a bit of optimism returned to the market, everything soared.

Keep in mind, when things are truly bad, you don't need them to get "good" to make a lot of money quickly. As my friend and colleague Steve Sjuggerud often points out, you make the big money as things go from "bad to less bad."

The greatest trader ever, George Soros, has a good quote about this... or at least it is attributed to him. He said, *The worse a situation becomes, the less it takes to turn it around, and the bigger the upside.*"

That's a great way to sum up crisis trading. When things are truly bad... and assets are truly cheap... just a tiny bit of optimism can produce giant investment gains.

Stansberry Research: Can this apply to individual companies?

Hunt: Absolutely. You can use a crisis to get a good deal on an individual company, as well. Warren Buffett is one of the world's greatest practitioners of buying in times of crisis. He comes off as a grandfatherly "aw, shucks" type of guy. But he's a stone-cold crisis hunter.

In 1964, he made a hugely successful investment in credit-card company American Express after it was rocked by a crisis.

American Express had extended loans to a company that was busted for falsifying documents. Its share price fell nearly 50%. Afterward, Buffett bought the stock. He ended up making a fortune and owning more than 10% of one of the all-time greatest American businesses.

Buffett was also an active buyer and lender during the 2008 credit crisis. He made a handful of spectacular investments during that time.

Buffett is famous for saying that he likes to invest in great companies that have been hit by a one-time huge, but solvable problem. In other words, he looks to buy great companies after a crisis.

Stansberry Research: It's obvious that you can earn big returns buying after a crisis. But it's very hard for people to take action.

Hunt: Yes. It is hard when you are starting out. As I mentioned, humans are hardwired to seek the safety of crowds. Fifty thousand years ago, it's how we survived.

But when it comes to investing and trading, you won't succeed doing what everyone else is doing. And during a crisis, almost everyone panics and sells. You must fight the natural instinct to run away from the crisis... and instead run toward it.

It's like any useful skill. You have to practice. After enough practice, it will get easier... and then it will become an automatic response.

When you're starting out, you can lean on the wisdom of investment masters like Warren Buffett and Nathan Rothschild.

One of the best things Buffett ever said was to succeed as an investor, *"You want to be greedy when others are fearful, and fearful when others are greedy."* You also have legendary financier Nathan Rothschild's recommendation: *"Buy when there is blood in the streets."*

To develop a useful crisis mindset, try this: **The next time you read awful headlines about an individual country or a stock market sector, go into the market and buy a small position in the beaten-up asset**. Buy $500 worth of stock.

You'll feel funny doing it. You might get a bad feeling in your stomach. That's actually a good sign that you're doing the right thing. After you do it enough... and make 50% or 100% in a year a few times, you'll develop an appreciation for a good crisis.

Stansberry Research: OK... let's say I buy after a crisis. What are the risks?

Hunt: The biggest risk is that the crisis turns into a long-lasting crisis. For example, a quick military flare up between two countries could turn into a full-blown war. A country's stock crash could turn into a bear market that lasts a long, long time.

That's why it pays to do a lot of research on what you are considering buying. You need to make sure you're buying quality businesses at good values. For example, if a sector experiences a crisis, I try to simply buy the best business in that sector.

You also need to employ risk-limiting techniques like position sizing, which is the part of your trading strategy that tells you how much of a position to buy. You don't want to take a position so large that you get really hurt if you're wrong.

You can also set a stop loss on your position, which is a predetermined point at which you will sell if the price moves against you.

Stansberry Research: Makes sense. Any parting thoughts?

Hunt: One last thing. I know it may sound heartless to talk about crises like this. I don't root for people to lose their jobs or suffer through bad times. But crisis situations are part of life. It's how the world works.

I didn't write the rules. I just play by them. And it happens that crisis situations often produce excellent trading and investing opportunities.

Realize It's Perfectly OK to DO NOTHING From Time to Time

Many people make terrible mistakes with their investments because they're always looking for "action."

They get impatient and buy an investment not because it's a great bargain, but because they just want to be doing something.

If you don't see any great values in the market, don't buy anything. It's perfectly OK to park your wealth in cash... and wait for great values to appear.

In the following chapter, you'll learn all about the "art of inaction."

The Power of Doing Nothing

By Porter Stansberry

Every Friday, Porter Stansberry uses his column in *The Stansberry Digest* e-letter to share investment wisdom he has picked up over the years as a financial publisher.

In this classic essay, Porter explains the power of inaction... and how to use it to your advantage as an investor...

———————•———————

In this letter, we'll discuss the importance of doing nothing. Yes, you read that right. I want you to learn how *not* to buy stocks... How *not* to trade commodities... How *not* to sell options or buy corporate bonds...

I'm going to show you the most important secret of all is learning to do nothing. In my Friday *Digest*, I do my best to tell you the things I'd want to know if our roles were reversed. Many of the things I've written to you about over the years are bad for my business. And nothing is worse for my business than advising you to do nothing...

That's why no one else in finance is going to tell you, the client, to do nothing. It's not in their interest for you to do nothing. We – the professional financial community – need you to do *something*. Anything. We need you to take action so we can sell you information and services. You don't need a broker unless you're going to make a trade. You don't need a newsletter to tell you to do nothing.

Now, let me explain why doing nothing is so important. Just look at the stock market chart on the next page...

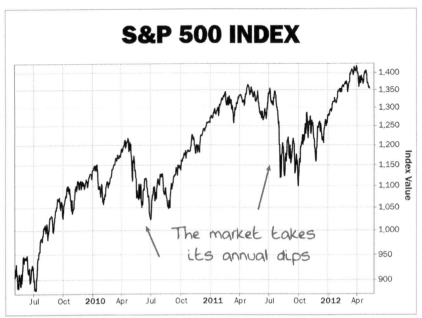

S&P 500 INDEX

The market takes its annual dips

Index Value

At some point each year, the stock market suddenly remembers that the world's financial system suffers from serious problems – namely, that those who back the system are mostly broke.

In 2010, the break came from April through early August. It featured a massive run into U.S. Treasury bonds and collapsing stock prices. The downtrends continued until Ben Bernanke, the Federal Reserve chairman, promised to print another trillion dollars in the second week of August.

At that moment, the prevailing downward trends completely reversed. Stocks went up. Commodities went up. And interest rates went up.

In 2011, the break came in August. Everything plummeted as the world suddenly realized that Europe's banks didn't have any money left. Once again, U.S. Treasury bonds rallied (interest rates fell), stocks plummeted across the board, commodities did a swan dive... and European bank stocks were beaten like rented mules.

This time, the European money printers came to the rescue. They promised to print in October (and actually began printing in December).

The result was a huge rally – across the board. It didn't matter what you bought in December 2011. Everything soared.

Hopefully, you see the pattern. The world's monetary authorities simply exchange the value we hold in our currency for value in financial assets (stocks and bonds) and commodities. It's a game that destroys the purchasing power of the working class' wages, while enriching the speculators and investors who know how to game the system.

How do you game the system? *Learn to do nothing.* What I mean is by 2012, the game became so rigged that various measures of the market's variability completely collapsed. All stocks, all bonds, all prices... everything... moved in lockstep. That's because all these prices are set in the paper that's printed in massive quantities.

Compared to the monetary forces at play, the things that normally drive stock prices – like interest rates and earnings – make almost no difference.

Your efforts to overcome this volatility by doing *something* – by hedging, by trading, by buying the "right" stock – are all likely to fail. No, that's not a guarantee. And yes, you can do a lot of powerful things to generate income that will help you weather these storms. But the most powerful thing you can do is *nothing.*

You see, while prices move together, *value* is widely variable. During a crisis, there's no difference between the best companies and the worst. They all sell off together. Therein lies a tremendous opportunity – if you've learned to do nothing.

Here's all you have to do: Pick three or four stocks you want to own. Look back and think of the companies you should have bought in previous years. Make sure they're the highest-quality names you can find. Set aside 5% of your net worth in cash for each of these names. Just sit on it. Don't worry about the yield you're losing. Don't trade the funds. Do nothing.

It's an extremely powerful feeling. You're going to take advantage of the market instead of being its victim. That's the secret of doing nothing.

How will you know when it's time to buy? Here are a few simple guidelines...

Imagine if you only bought stocks when:

1. The Volatility Index ("VIX") – the so-called "fear gauge," which measures put premiums – is over 30.

2. Stocks have fallen by at least 15% on the S&P 500 and/or 20% on the Nasdaq.

3. A friend or a relative calls in a panic and asks what to do about his investments.

4. You don't want to pick up the newspaper or turn on CNBC because you know the news is going to be terrible.

If you're prepared... you won't be worried. If you've picked the stocks you're going to buy ahead of time, you won't doubt yourself. You won't be acting out of fear or greed or panic. You have a plan. You've learned to do nothing... until it's time to buy. You'll know when it's time. It'll be obvious.

If you can learn to do nothing... the market's volatility and the giant rigged game we call the world's monetary system ceases to be a problem. It becomes a giant opportunity. Learning to do nothing takes all the power back from the market and gives it to you.

I encourage you to start small...

I know that if you try things on a small scale – like shorting one share of stock, buying a single bond, or selling one put contract – you can mitigate almost all the downside and nearly all the fear. It's scary doing things for the first time with your own money.

The way to overcome this paralyzing fear... and the only way to learn to become a better investor... is to start small and get some experience. Learning to do nothing is harder than it looks. And it's far more powerful than you'll likely realize until you start doing it.

You'll be constantly tempted to do something with the cash you're sitting on. So start small. Then... as the strategy works... you'll want to do it more and with more of your assets.

Anaconda Trading

An interview with Dr. David Eifrig, Jr.

Dr. David Eifrig is an expert at finding low-risk, high-reward investment opportunities safe enough for even the most risk-averse investor.

Below, "Doc" shares his own spin on the art of inaction – what he calls "anaconda trading."

Whether you're just getting started with investing or on the verge of retirement, this idea could dramatically increase your returns while saving you a huge amount of time and money.

———————●———————

Stansberry Research: Doc, your advisories – *Retirement Millionaire* and *Retirement Trader* – are centered around an idea you call "anaconda trading." Can you define this idea for us?

Dr. David Eifrig: Sure... First, "anaconda trading" doesn't pertain to a particular trading strategy. Instead, it's a framework to think about trading and investing. It's how many of the world's richest and most successful investors grow and protect their wealth.

I realize it might seem like a silly comparison, but I've found the most useful way to describe this approach is in terms of the anaconda. Anacondas are the largest snakes in the world. And they're one of the deadliest, most efficient predators... but they don't hunt like most other animals.

Anacondas don't "zip" around chasing after their prey. They don't get into long battles with them. In fact, they don't hunt in a traditional sense at all.

Instead, they lie around in rivers for long periods of time. They wait for an unsuspecting animal to pass by or stop for a drink of water. Only then do they strike... by slowly wrapping themselves around the prey and holding on until the animal stops breathing. Then, with their large mouth, they swallow their prey whole. It's a unique strategy in nature. They're nature's "cheap shot" artists.

Said another way, anacondas aren't interested in fair fights...
They'll only strike when the odds are overwhelmingly on their side.
They're "no risk" operators. They take their time waiting for their
prey and, once it's captured, waiting for the capture to pay off.

Anacondas can grow to a huge size because they don't spend
much time or energy chasing every animal that comes along.

Stansberry Research: How do you apply this idea to investing?

Eifrig: Well, that's how the world's best investors think about
buying stocks, bonds, and commodities. They act only when the
odds are heavily stacked in their favor. In a similar way, their
portfolios can grow to enormous size because they're greatly
reducing risk.

If you begin to think about investing this way, you can avoid a
huge amount of worry and wasted time, and set yourself up to
make extraordinary returns. Like the anaconda, you can rest
along the river bank until the right opportunity presents itself.

Stansberry Research: Can you give us an example of how
you've used this approach?

Eifrig: Sure, a great example was in 2010 when bank analyst
Meredith Whitney went on *60 Minutes* and predicted hundreds
of billions of dollars of losses in the municipal bond market.
Muni bonds collapsed in price, but I thought it was a major
overreaction... the predictions were factually incorrect.

So we were able to buy these bonds at a major discount with
little risk, simply by waiting for a fantastic opportunity to come to
us. And we made great, safe returns over the next several years.

Stansberry Research: How about an example of how this idea
applies to shorter-term trading?

Eifrig: One of my favorite ways to use this idea for trading is to
take advantage of spikes in volatility. The Volatility Index, also
known as the "VIX" or "fear index," tends to rise as stocks fall
and investors become more fearful.

The VIX is also used to determine option prices... When
volatility spikes, options become more expensive. Yet these
periods of high volatility typically don't last long... and as any
professional trader will tell you, most options expire worthless.

So when we occasionally see a big spike in volatility, it often makes sense to sell – essentially short-sell – puts on stocks you'd like to own anyway. The ins and outs of selling puts are beyond the scope of this interview, but this is an ideal "anaconda" situation.

One of the best examples of this is the stock crash of late 2008 and early 2009. Investors who were patient and prudent were able to collect a huge amount of low-risk income and pick up some of the world's best companies at absurdly cheap prices.

Stansberry Research: Are there any risks or hurdles with "anaconda trading?"

Eifrig: Because it's a framework rather than a specific strategy, **there aren't really risks in the traditional sense. Followed prudently, it can only help you.** It's a simple idea, but it can be difficult for the novice investor to apply consistently. You'll learn patience and discipline.

Few people are naturally wired with the patience required to be successful investors. It's often just the opposite. Many investors act as though frequent buying and selling is the ticket to huge wealth. But it's exactly this behavior that ensures the average investor will never build real wealth through investing.

It doesn't help that Wall Street does all it can to encourage this behavior – that's where the commissions are made – and the financial media are constantly talking about the latest hot stock picks.

For most people, this is something they have to work at... a skill they have to build. But it's one of the best things you can do to improve your investing and trading results immediately. I recommend everyone give it a try.

Stansberry Research: Thanks for talking with us, Doc.

Eifrig: You're welcome.

Realize Wall Street Isn't in the Business of Helping Individuals. It's in the Business of Making Money.

Wall Street bankers drive around in $200,000 cars, live in $10 million homes, and build hugely expensive corporate headquarters.

The money required for all that comes from customers who are encouraged to buy every piece-of-crap security the bankers can come up with. It's the same way that Las Vegas casino owners get rich.

Wall Street is in the business of raising money for its corporate clients. It does this by structuring stock and bond deals... and then collecting huge banking fees when investors buy them. Some of these deals are good for individual investors... but MANY are not.

Think about the brokers, lawyers, accountants, and other people you do business with. Always ask what they get out of it. Ask what has to happen for them to make money. When you buy stocks, ask who's selling them or who has sold you on the idea of buying them. **Know the business you're in, and know the businesses you deal with**.

In Concept 9, you'll learn what most brokers and financial advisors won't tell you – starting with the hidden truth about the way Wall Street works... and a few ways you can start protecting yourself...

The Only Chance You've Got to Be a Successful Investor

By Porter Stansberry

I'm going to tell you an unpleasant truth...

Most of you reading this will not make money with your investments this year... or next year. Most of you, in all likelihood, will never make money in the stock market.

It may shock you to hear it. It might make you angry. It might fill you with strong doubts about my credibility.

I'm telling you anyway because I'm convinced the only chance you've got to become a successful investor is to start by acknowledging that reality. Once you know that individual investors generally fare poorly in stocks, you can begin to examine why...

We know from Dalbar – a Boston-based consultancy that studies actual mutual-fund returns – that most individual investors don't make money in the stock market.

We know from the investment management firm BlackRock, whose study is shown on the next page...

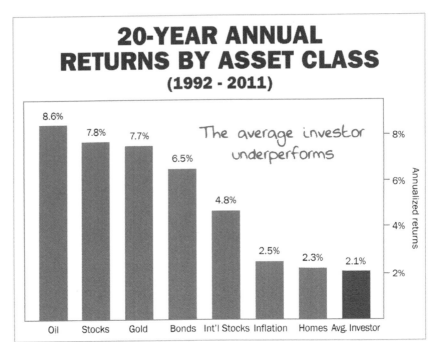

20-YEAR ANNUAL RETURNS BY ASSET CLASS (1992 - 2011)

The average investor underperforms

8.6%	7.8%	7.7%	6.5%	4.8%	2.5%	2.3%	2.1%
Oil	Stocks	Gold	Bonds	Int'l Stocks	Inflation	Homes	Avg. Investor

Source: BlackRock

We also know from discussions with dozens of certified public accountants that almost all their clients lose money in their personal brokerage accounts.

Why?

Let's start with the most obvious reason: **The financial industry does not exist because it enriches its clients. The clients provide all the wealth required to maintain the financial industry.**

The profits that power the branding and the marketing of mutual-fund companies and big investment banks came out of the pockets of their clients. Think about that. Think about it carefully the next time you consider following any financial institution's advice about what to do with your savings.

Investment banks exist to raise capital for corporate clients. They do not exist to give you a good stock tip or put you in a safe bond. (If you need a refresher course on the way Wall Street really works, read the famous book *Liar's Poker*.)

The other main reason people, on average, tend to fare so poorly in stocks is that few individual investors know anything about how to value a security – a stock or a bond.

Let me give you a vital tip: If you don't know more about the value of something than the person who is selling it to you, the chances of you profiting from the transaction are extremely close to zero.

At Stansberry Research, we've written volumes about how to value stocks and bonds. But... the writing is "boring." It requires careful thought and attention. Most people, it seems, would rather trust some lines on a chart...

Yes, sometimes these guides will work. But if you believe charts can compensate for a complete lack of basic financial skills... you will soon go broke in the stock market. That, my friends, is a fact. If you don't know how to value the business you're about to invest in, don't make the investment.

The last nail in the coffin of the failed individual investor is a complete lack of risk management.

Catastrophic losses happen for the same reason, every time. They don't happen because an investment idea didn't work out. Even great investors are only going to be right about stocks roughly 60% of the time. Catastrophic losses happen because people can't stand to take small losses. They allow them to grow into big losses.

There are two good ways to make sure this never happens to you. The first way is completely foolproof: **Never invest more in any individual stock than you're OK losing**. If it goes down 100%, it shouldn't matter to your financial well-being. That means if you're investing a total portfolio of $100,000... you'll limit your position sizes to $2,000 (or maybe $5,000 at the most).

Worst-case scenario, you lose 5% of your portfolio. That's not going to kill you. With some kinds of companies (risky biotechs and mining stocks, for example), this is the only kind of risk-management technique that really works because the shares are too volatile for trailing stops...

The other way to prevent catastrophic losses is to simply decide, in advance, when you will sell. It might be on the basis of negative price action (a trailing stop). Or it might be at a fixed price – you'll sell if shares drop to less than $10, for example. Or you can use charts to find points where you no longer want to risk owning the stock.

I don't really care what kind of risk management you use... so long as you use something. **I can guarantee that if you don't have your risk strategy figured out, sooner or later, you will suffer a catastrophic loss... and it will completely wipe out all your previous gains**. That's just what happens.

This is the most important information I can possibly give you.

You need to realize that most investors will fail. You need to understand why they fail and how they fail. They fail because they allow their emotions to overtake their reason. They fail because they don't have the most basic tools – they don't know how to value stocks. And they fail because they eventually suffer a catastrophic loss.

I truly hope you'll take this essay to heart. I hope you'll look back on the investment mistakes you've made and think about why they happened. It wasn't just because you bought the wrong stock.

Find a way to eliminate these mistakes, and you'll be on your way to becoming a more successful investor.

Why Your Broker Knowingly Gets You into Losing Trades

By Brian Hunt

Wall Street is full of conflicting interests. So the vast majority of Wall Street research is unreliable.

That may go against everything you've ever been told about the market. But as Stansberry Research Editor in Chief Brian Hunt says in the following essay, following Wall Street stock ratings is one of the "surest paths in the world to wrecking your portfolio."

Read on to learn how to make far more money than the average investor... and avoid being "Wall Street's patsy"...

———————•———————

If you've been investing for more than a few years, you've likely taken comfort in the idea of buying a stock that is highly rated by Wall Street analysts.

You might have heard something like, "19 out of 20 analysts that cover the company rate it as a buy." You probably felt good you owned shares in a company that so many other people liked.

You might factor in rosy Wall Street analyst ratings when looking for new stock purchases.

This belief is widespread. Almost every "armchair investor" in America has it...

And it's one of the surest paths in the world to wrecking your portfolio.

Buying stocks with high ratings from lots of Wall Street analysts should be nicknamed, "Getting in way too late"... or "Holding the bag."

If you're buying stocks that are rated "buys" from "19 out of 20 analysts," congratulations. You're Wall Street's patsy.

A stock market participant will make far more money by focusing on ideas that are ignored – or even hated – by the majority of Wall Street analysts. By taking this approach, you'll get far more value for your investment dollar. You'll avoid being Wall Street's patsy.

There are two major reasons the vast majority of Wall Street research is unreliable...

One: Although many Wall Street analysts have expensive degrees and excellent training, they are ultimately humans. We're social creatures. It feels good to be part of a crowd.

Often, the desire to be part of a crowd overwhelms the good sense of even the smartest people. So even though an analyst might think a certain stock or a certain industry sector is a great bargain, he will be hesitant to say "Buy!" if many other people have doubts about the idea. It's going to be too uncomfortable for the analyst.

The problem here is that an "investment crowd" is almost always wrong. When everyone loves an idea, it's going to be a terrible bargain. Optimistic bidders will have already pushed shares to excessive valuations. New buyers get a horrible deal. They buy expensive shares from the folks who got in early... And they get soaked.

Two: Wall Street makes the bulk of its profits not from providing great research... but from doing things like raising money for companies and collecting fees.

Wall Street has a vested interest in the public staying relentlessly positive. When the public is relentlessly positive, it relentlessly buys stocks and bonds. This creates billions and billions of dollars in profit for Wall Street.

For example, if a firm is raising money for a steel maker, you can be sure that its analysts will be encouraged to write positive reports about the steel industry... no matter what they really think. The analysts have to "toe the company line."

The average investor doesn't give much thought to this... but it's common knowledge in the industry. Insiders know that most Wall Street research is created to fleece ignorant investors. When you buy a stock because it is highly rated by Wall Street firms, it's like buying a used car that is rated highly by the majority of used-car salesmen on the lot.

For example... during the late-1990s tech bull market, Wall Street analysts placed "buy" ratings on hundreds of companies that had no shot at making money. But those companies were paying Wall Street billions of dollars in fees. In private e-mails, analysts called the companies "pieces of s**t," while urging small investors to load up.

In 2007, just before the credit crash, Wall Street analysts had almost every mortgage-related security rated as a "buy." It was in their interest to convince investors to buy this toxic stuff. Wall Street was earning billions of dollars selling it to the public.

These are recent examples... But these conflicts of interest have existed for a hundred years.

Again... you're far better off focusing on companies and sectors that the majority of Wall Street analysts are ignoring... or are even extremely bearish on. Buying assets that Wall Street analysts can't stand will get you into situations like buying cheap, ignored gold stocks in 2001... right before they entered a massive bull market.

Adopting this strategy will feel strange at first. You'll be doing the opposite of what "experts" on television are telling you to do. It will be uncomfortable to be away from the crowd.

But remember... those experts are subject to mindless, crowd-following urges like anyone else. They also make the most money by selling the most dangerous assets. They are the high-priced equivalent of a used-car salesman knowingly selling you a lemon... while raving about its performance.

— Concept 10 —

Resolve to Avoid Complex Investments You Don't Understand

Great investments aren't complicated. They are often very simple. Wall Street doesn't want you to know this because – as we discussed in Concept 9 – it wants you to be dependent on its "genius."

Before you buy a single stock, go buy a pack of index cards. If you can't describe on an index card why it makes sense to buy an investment, pass on it. Don't buy it. Something simple and safe will come around soon.

The following story will show you exactly why this is so important to your investment success. In this chapter – the 10th concept of successful wealth building and investment – Dan Ferris shares the unfortunate story of Henry Gribbohm. According to Dan, understanding the plight of "Poor Henry" can help you avoid the four common mistakes investors make...

107

The Four Common Mistakes Investors Make

By Dan Ferris

"Tubs of Fun" is a simple carnival game.

You throw a softball into a plastic tub from a few feet away. The object is to make the ball stay in the tub.

It sounds easy, but it's not. The ball is too bouncy, and the tub is too hard. It's difficult to keep the ball from bouncing out of the tub. The player has the illusion he's throwing a ball into a container. But he's really just throwing it at a solid wall.

To make it worse, the worker running the game lets you take a practice throw. First he drops a softball in the tub, and it stays, because he's standing right next to the tub. Then you throw a softball, and the ball he dropped in absorbs the energy from the one you threw, and your ball stays, too. But when you play for real money, you can only throw the ball into an empty tub.

If you're not the sharpest tool in the shed, you won't figure this trick out.

But hey, it's a carnival game. Everybody knows you're not supposed to win. Right? Well, no. Not everybody...

Enter 30-year-old Henry Gribbohm, a tough-looking, tattooed young man with a toddler to care for and $2,600 in cash burning holes in the pockets of his dusty work pants.

On a recent spring day, Gribbohm walked into the Fiesta Shows traveling carnival in Epsom, New Hampshire. He walked out shortly after, his pockets empty, with a large stuffed banana toy with a smiley face and a dreadlocks haircut draped across the top of his toddler's stroller. A news reporter said the funky banana toy was worth $149.

Gribbohm watched the worker do his little practice throw routine and didn't figure out the ruse. So Gribbohm played and played... He lost $300 within minutes. He went home and fetched another $2,300, all that remained of his life savings. He returned to the game and lost all that, too.

He admitted on camera, "You get caught up in the whole double-or-nothing-I've-got-to-win-my-money-back..."

The thing is... many investors are walking in Gribbohm's shoes... They're making exactly the same mistakes...

Gribbohm's first mistake was ignorance of the game he was playing.

Gribbohm was on a financial mission. He started playing Tubs of Fun to win a Microsoft Xbox Kinect video game device (valued at $100). When his first attempts were unsuccessful, he ran home, got more money, and kept at it.

Gribbohm later filed charges against the game owner, alleging fraud.

Yes, Henry Gribbohm thinks alleging a carnival game was fixed is a plausible defense for being clueless enough to give $2,600 away voluntarily. He kept plowing money into a carnival game... while being totally ignorant of the fact that carnival games are rigged.

You might think Gribbohm is uniquely naive. But millions of investors are just as bad as he is. They have no idea that Wall Street is often about the same as a carnival.

Wall Street is in the business of selling stocks and bonds. This business generates billions of dollars in fees. It's a business that allows bankers to drive around in $300,000 cars... afford $10 million homes in the Hamptons... and collect absurd bonuses. That money comes from customers who are encouraged to buy every piece-of-crap security the bankers can come up with.

Think about the brokers, lawyers, accountants, and other people you do business with. Always ask what they get out of it. Ask what has to happen for them to make money. When you buy stocks, ask who's selling them, or who has sold you on the idea of buying them. Know the business you're in, and know the businesses you deal with.

Gribbohm's second mistake was pursuing easy financial gain.

Most people don't understand that easy financial gain is one of the worst things that can happen to them. Ask a lottery winner. According to author Don McNay's book, *Life Lessons from the*

Lottery, the lives of lottery winners are usually a wreck within about five years of winning.

Lottery winners get a ton of money they didn't earn without any practice at hanging onto large sums of money. It's really, really hard to do that. It's like ordering a drink at your favorite watering hole and being dropped into a giant vat of beer.

Technically speaking, you got what you asked for... just more. More is bad when you're not prepared for it... when you didn't do more to earn it.

Aspiring to easy financial gain might be normal, but it's also self-destructive. Gribbohm was trying to win a $100 prize by playing a $2 carnival game. His results speak for themselves.

Investors make this same mistake as well. They buy risky options and hot tips from friends in the pursuit of fast, easy gains. They see the stock market as a lottery... rather than a place where one can buy pieces of world-class businesses that they can hold for decades.

Gribbohm's next big mistake was giving in to a bias toward action.

Nobody likes to sit still. And that's too bad.

Famous 17th-century French mathematician and scientist Blaise Pascal said, "All men's miseries derive from not being able to sit in a quiet room alone."

If you search for Gribbohm's picture on Google, you'll see that he's a tough-looking guy. You can imagine him giving in to pressure to "act like a man." Men don't refrain from action. Men act. They take dramatic and constant action. When the going gets tough, the tough get – you get the picture.

People think "doing something" is always the answer. Nobody thinks doing nothing is the answer.

On the flip side, the actions that keep you from losing at the carnival and in the market will not impress other tough guys, nor attract women looking for tough guys.

Taking big risks is more likely to make you feel like a swaggering gambler, someone who's "not afraid to risk it all on a roll of the dice." It'll at least attract a fair amount of attention.

Henry Gribbohm got plenty of attention!

I've said before that fear is the dominant emotion in the market at all times. When it appears greed has taken over, it's really just the fear of being left out. That fear drives people to constantly seek action.

The final mistake Gribbohm made was not knowing how far he was going to go.

Gribbohm's story shows you how crazy financial decisions can get, especially when speculating on great financial gain. He lost because he couldn't trust himself. He didn't decide beforehand how he'd behave if presented with a game like Tubs of Fun.

What will you do if the stock market falls? What are your goals? I can't really answer any of those questions, but I can tell you what I'll do. I'm a dedicated lifetime buyer of equities. I do what I believe is enough homework to know which stocks to buy and which ones to avoid.

Other things being equal, when the market falls, I buy more of what I like, same as I do when chocolate-chip cookies go on sale at the grocery store. I want more cookies, so I like it when my money buys more of them. I like equity returns, too, so I really like it when my dollar buys bigger ones.

Every stock investor faces a list of huge unknowns. You're not in control of stock prices or interest rates or tomorrow's headlines. You must make your own behavior in the stock market the most solid, reliable of known entities. You must be in control of yourself.

At any point during his incredible losing streak, Gribbohm could have wised up and walked away... but he didn't.

Many investors make the same mistakes he did. If you're one of them, wise up and walk away. And before you come back, make sure you learn the game you're playing.

To Learn More About Smart Investing...

Consider the ideas in this book as "Investing 101." And now that you've mastered the bare essentials, it's time to take the next step...

In the following essay, Stansberry Research editor Dan Ferris shares his recommended reading list for new investors.

These books will not only give you a look into the strategies and ideas of some of the world's greatest investment minds... they'll also provide more detail on ideas like how to value a business, how to start your search for great investments, and even how to save money.

Better yet, these books combined will cost you less than $100 on Amazon... and much less if you buy them used. **After reading the books on this list, you will be ahead of 99.9% of your fellow investors...**

A World-Class Investment Education for Less Than $100

By Dan Ferris

If you search "investing" on Amazon's book list, you'll get more than 70,000 results.

But here's what Amazon – and almost no one else – will tell you about your search...

More than 99% of the investing books out there aren't worth the time it takes to read them.

Some books are just magazine articles that book publishers expanded into hundreds of pages of fluff. Some books are academic blather that doesn't apply to the real world. Some books are OK, but they can't hold a candle to the best ones. They aren't worth your time.

This is a major problem for people who want a basic investment education.

You want to build a foundation of basic stock market knowledge, but with tens of thousands of titles out there, where do you start?

Below is a list of the best, easy-to-read books on how to identify great businesses... how much you should pay for them... and how you can use them to safely compound your wealth for a long, long time.

If you're someone who realizes the power of education, I've written this list for you.

- The first investing book I recommend anyone read is _The Elements of Investing_, by Burton Malkiel and Charles Ellis.

  This is the only book I've encountered on the basics of investing that begins with the correct first investment topic: saving money.

  Hanging onto a big sum of money without blowing it is by far the single most important investment skill of them all.

That is the one skill without which you simply can never be an investor.

Other essential topics in the book include compounding, diversification, avoiding blunders, and keeping your investment strategy simple.

From cover to cover, every word of this book is essential reading for the novice stock market investor looking to start out on the right foot.

- Then be sure to read Peter Lynch's book, *One Up on Wall Street*.

  It'll teach you how to think about the overall stock market and how to spot good businesses to buy.

  Lynch is famous for encouraging investors to buy what they understand. For example, just about anyone can go to the grocery store and look around at various products, comparing those he likes with those he doesn't like.

- Lynch's next book, *Beating the Street*, is great, too. It goes into detail about specific industries – like retail, real estate, savings and loans, cyclical industries, and restaurants.

  Lynch also offers his 25 golden rules of investing, which are incredibly valuable.

- Now you're ready to get to the nitty gritty of business valuation.

  Start with Joel Greenblatt's *The Little Book That Still Beats the Market*. It's easy to read and easy to understand.

  It'll teach you a simple investment approach that boils down to: Buy good businesses, but only at cheap prices.

- Then read Joe Ponzio's *F Wall Street*. This is a must-read mostly on the strength of the second section, called "How to Approach Investing from a Business Perspective."

  It has a great chapter called "How to Value a Business." This chapter boils business valuation down to two core sources of value creation (cash flow and net worth).

  Ponzio says simply that if a business isn't causing one or

both of these sources of value creation to increase, forget it and move on. That's great advice. You don't want to waste time with a business that's shrinking.

- Frank Singer's little book, _How to Value a Business_, teaches you a simple formula for business valuation. It also shows you the simple math that explains why a business is worth so much more to a so-called "strategic acquirer" than it is to anybody else.

  (For example, global confectionery manufacturer Mars buying candy maker Wrigley in 2008 was a strategic acquisition because it improved Mars' position in the candy market.)

- Lastly, I recommend Greenblatt's _You Can Be a Stock Market Genius_. It has specific approaches that show you how to find great stocks. It's where I learned about the value of spinoffs... when a company distributes the stock of a subsidiary, making it into a separate publicly traded company.

The book covers other types of stocks, too. It's considered required reading in the hedge-fund industry.

Keep in mind: There are a few other great investment books out there. Chapters 8 and 20 of Ben Graham's _The Intelligent Investor_ and Warren Buffett's Berkshire Hathaway letters are world-class educational material.

But the above list will get you started on the right path. It's a list focused on the best, easy-to-read books that explain how to identify and value great businesses. You can buy all of them new for less than $100... and much less if you buy them used.

If you're interested in building long-term wealth in stocks, read these books and forget the rest.

Further Resources

To follow along with Stansberry Research's top investment recommendations and further your education, consider subscribing to our following newsletters...

- ***True Wealth*** is written by Dr. Steve Sjuggerud. Steve has seen the investment business from a handful of different angles. He has worked as a stock broker, became the vice president of a $50 million international mutual fund, worked for two billion-dollar hedge funds, and earned a Ph.D. in finance.

Since 2001, Steve has been focused on *True Wealth*, one of the most widely-read investment letters in America and more than 125 countries. In short, Steve specializes in finding safe, alternative ways to make big gains, without taking big risks. His contrarian philosophy led him to close the highest-returning position in the history of Stansberry Research.

To learn more about *True Wealth* and how to sign up, type this unique, safe, and secure website address into your Internet browser: www.sbry.co/fnjnxW.

- **Retirement Millionaire** is written by Dr. David Eifrig. "Doc" (as we call him) has actually retired twice... once as a Wall Street derivatives trader and again as an eye surgeon.

  His *Retirement Millionaire* service covers everything from great long-term investments... safe income from high-quality businesses... and unconventional investments you'll never hear about in the mainstream media.

Doc also shares unusual ways to save money in retirement... debunks many of the myths you've been told about mainstream medicine... and provides great alternative health tips in every issue.

To learn more about *Retirement Millionaire* and how to sign up, type this unique, safe, and secure website address into your Internet browser: www.sbry.co/9SlWsj.

More from
Stansberry Research

The World's Greatest Investment Ideas

The Stansberry Research Trader's Manual

The Doctor's Protocol Field Manual

*High Income Retirement:
How to Safely Earn 12% to 20%
Income Streams on Your Savings*

*World Dominating Dividend Growers:
Income Streams That Never Go Down*

*Secrets of the Natural Resource Market:
How to Set Yourself up for Huge Returns
in Mining, Energy, and Agriculture*

The Stansberry Research Guide to Investment Basics

*The Living Cure:
The Promise of Cancer Immunotherapy*

97458947R00075

Made in the USA
Middletown, DE
05 November 2018